KOMSOMOL PARTICIPATION IN THE SOVIET FIRST FIVE-YEAR PLAN

Komsomol Participation in the Soviet First Five-Year Plan

Ann Todd Baum

St. Martin's Press   New York

First published in the United States of America in 1987

Printed in Hong Kong

ISBN 0–312–00786–8

Library of Congress Cataloging-in-Publication Data
Baum, Ann Todd.
Komsomol participation in the Soviet first
five-year plan.
Bibliography: p.
Includes index.
1. Vsesoíûznyĭ leninskiĭ kommunisticheskiĭ
soíûz molodezhi—History.   2. Soviet Union—
Economic policy—1928–1932.   I. Title.
HS3260.S654V7432   1987   330.947′0842   87–4284
ISBN 0–312–00786–8

To the memory of my grandfather
Grover Cleveland Todd, Sr

Contents

Acknowledgements

I wish to thank my mother, Verdie Todd, for her optimism, and my father, Grover Todd, for always urging me to do things the 'right way'. To my husband Dale, I give heartfelt thanks for tolerating my lapses of humour and for his calming influence. Patricia Stranahan and Betty M. Unterberger provided invaluable editorial advice at different stages of this project, as did Chester A. Dunning, Roger Beaumont, and Arnold P. Krammer. John D. Robertson was unfailingly supportive and enthusiastic in his guidance and direction. Ralph T. Fisher and the staff of the Slavic and East European Studies Institute of the University of Illinois were extremely courteous and helpful during crucial periods of research. Woody Smith and Ralph J. Q. Adams provided training and technical advice. Susan D. Roberts, Katherine O'Keefe, and Dennis Berthold inspired me with confidence and friendship, as well as a desire to learn. Patricia Tollison helped make this book a reality by giving me the courage to let it happen. Finally, my deepest appreciation must go to my friend and mentor, Candida J. Lutes, and to my ever-faithful companion, Beauregard Baum.

A.T.B.

List of Abbreviations and Acronyms

Abbreviations

ROTC	Reserve Officer Training Corps
NEP	New Economic Policy
USSR	United Soviet Socialist Republics
GTO	Ready for Labour and Defence Test

Acronyms

Narkompros	Commissariat for the Enlightenment
Rabfak	Workers' faculty
VUZy	University
FZY	Factory school

Introduction

Established political systems often use socialization techniques to transfer values to younger generations. In the United States, the Boy Scouts, Girl Scouts, Young Republicans, Young Democrats, Junior ROTC, and other student or youth groups attempt to inculcate their members with basic American principles. Such organizations are actually programmes designed to produce future leaders who can be relied upon to maintain the political status quo within acceptable parameters. Occasionally, the youthful portion of a population becomes so united and driven by an idea, an image of the future, that it transcends a mere socialization process and acquires a life of its own. In these circumstances youth movements are born.

Youth movements have been relatively common in many countries; their activities often mirror the underlying currents of political systems. A careful study of the activities of American Boy Scouts during World War II (a high-flux time for patriotic energy) would reveal interesting if not predictable patterns of political allegiance and behaviour. Similarly, examination of a comparable group in the Soviet Union during the First Five-Year Plan exposes processes unique to that system at that time. The most important youth group in Soviet Russia during the years 1928–33 was the Komsomol, an acronym for Communist Youth League (*Kommunisticheskii Soiuz Molodezhi*). Before examining the Komsomol, it is helpful to review several established cross-cultural theories concerning youth and youth movements, with specific reference to the period of adolescence.

The term adolescent, according to one authority, refers to the interim behaviour between childhood and adulthood. It is a condition marked by uncertainty and confusion to such an extent as to be synonymous with the term 'identity crisis'. Adolescence is in this context somewhat of a malady; in many cases extremely painful. It can lead to discomforting feelings of frustration, lack of direction, and isolation.[1] This has in recent history been shown to be especially common in urban-industrialized countries with stratified societies. In these situations, young people frequently feel left out. They often have a great deal of energy, but no place to direct it.

1

Some psychologists agree that the best 'cure' for the pains of adolescence is the development of a sense of identity, often achieved through intense ideological commitment and an environment providing guidance, fellowship, and a sense of belonging. Given this set of conditions, a feeling of meaningful belonging is created, and the symptoms of adolescence are minimized.[2]

The problems associated with adolescence in the Soviet Union were compounded by a unique situation which existed by 1928. After years of drift, in 1928 the country was on the verge of a crash industrialization programme, the First Five-Year Plan. This era has been referred to as the 'Stalin Revolution'.[3] Some historians suggest that the Stalin Revolution was in fact a continuation of the Russian Revolution which began October 1917, and was temporarily halted due to Lenin's New Economic Policy. Despite an acute lack of technology, skilled workers, and food, 1928 brought alarming revolutionary change during which Stalin, having consolidated his position, began ruthlessly dragging his country into the twentieth century. One fact has often been overlooked: in order to achieve his outrageous goals of rapid industrialization and modernization, Stalin needed a great deal of cooperation from those beneath him. The bulk of the population, the peasants, were reticent to contribute to his effort. The peaceful years of the New Economic Policy, Lenin's plan for withdrawing from the harsh measures of war communism, had allowed many peasants to reach a standard of living which was comfortable and economically secure. Some were actually wealthy, and later labelled 'kulaks'. When Stalin decided that Russia needed to marshal its resources and attempt a 200 per cent increase in production, relying on surpluses in agriculture to invest in rapid industrialization, he viewed the kulaks as an impediment to the process. In order to make the big push in industry, the urban workers had to eat. That food (substantial amounts) had to come from the countryside, and it had to come cheaply. By 1928 when the workers were clamouring for the state to provide them with grain, the peasants balked and withheld grain for higher prices. Peasants who had followed the party line during NEP and become involved in market practices, had since begun to enjoy self-sufficiency and comfortable profit margins. The notion of joining collective farms and rendering surplus to the cities, with little or no visible profit for the farmer, held no appeal. Stalin was enraged with peasant recalcitrance, and cast about for a way to displace 'peasant hoarders'. He seized upon the youth, the only sizeable segment of Russian society with the energy to carry out what amounted to a full-fledged ideological war.

Stalin's timing was perfect. The young people who considered themselves among the movers and shakers in the Soviet Union had since 1918 been effectively organized into the Komsomol, the youthful counterpart of the Bolshevik party. The group took itself seriously and desperately wanted to play an active part in the revolution. The Komsomolites' eagerness was of a complex nature. Not only did most of them believe in the principles of a Communist revolution, they also knew that through dedication they could make those principles become a working reality. Komsomol members were for the most part very ambitious and perceived participation in the League as a ticket to the top. The combination of these factors made the Komsomol a perfect candidate organization for the new revolutionary 'army' which Stalin needed to deliver socialist agriculture and do away with all obstacles to progress. Accordingly, in 1927 Stalin directed his propaganda machine to deluge the country with a war crisis rhetoric, creating a paranoia of the west and a general siege mentality.[4] He began issuing numerous letters in *Pravda*, the official party newspaper, which urged the youth to take up arms and become combat-ready to make the big push for modernization. By 1928 the Komsomol had filled its own newspaper, *Komsomol'skaia Pravda*, with similar exhortations. Content analysis of *Komsomol'skaia Pravda* reveals that this move was effective, especially in the year 1928, when initiation of action was vital.

By 1931, well into the First Five-Year Plan, western journals such as *Soviet Union Review* were reporting that tremendous gains had been achieved in the Soviet Union, especially in the fields of education and industry. These articles were in agreement with *Komsomol'skaia Pravda* and *Pravda* in suggesting that the Plan had achieved its goals thusfar in productivity and education. Since no other group had been involved in such as intense concerted effort, supported by approval from the Party and fuelled by incessant propaganda, it is reasonable to assume that many of the achievements of this process should be credited to the Komsomol. Western analysis of the First Five-Year Plan has for the most part not given adequate attention to the role played by the Komsomol.

During the First Five-Year Plan, virtually every line of propaganda from official sources was gathered toward stimulating industrialization. The goal was to mobilize the masses to the successful completion of the Plan. Under the direction of Stalin, the propaganda administration was skilful in its attempts to marshal the country's most dynamic element, the youth. The 'imagery of war' during the First Five-Year Plan symbolized a return to the spirit of battle.[5] For young men and women who had missed the chance at glory during the revolution or civil war and were disillusioned with the compromises of NEP, this propaganda was markedly appealing. The Komsomol systematically formed 'light brigades' in military fashion, and marched to the tune which Stalin set. Stalin had perceived the potential of the Komsomol, and he calculated that military jargon would be a persuasive tool in tapping that potential.

The propaganda which appeared in *Pravda* up to and including 1928, is important to this study, as well as that which is found in *Komsomol'skaia Pravda*. Both papers were oriented toward eliciting total loyalty and cooperation from young people. Agitation and propaganda had received special attention in the 1920s, when energy was needed to restore the shattered economic and political structures of the country. In 1921, the 'agitprop' department of the Communist Party became official and was defined as an 'instrument through which the Central Committee was to unite and direct all of the party's efforts in the realm of oral and printed propaganda and agitation'. It was assigned to guide the party's ideological work, especially in the field of political education.[6]

Actions of the Komsomol during the 1920s revealed a deep commitment to political education. By the time it held its Congress of 1926, the league had a total of 76 newspapers with a weekly output of 1 000 000 copies. Foremost among them was *Komsomol'skaia Pravda*, which had been founded as a daily paper on 24 May 1925.[7] The majority of the articles in these newspapers dealt with party ideology, and considering the extent of output, they must be regarded as an important tool of political education and socialization.

Beginning in 1928, *Komsomol'skaia Pravda* began gearing up for the 'big push' to industrialize and modernize Russia. It featured seemingly endless columns on the goals of the party and the opportunities for youth to participate. Entries on Marxism–Leninism were given new meaning in the context of sacrifice and struggle. Especially emphasized were the 'Subbotninki', the 'Saturday Workers', who gave their free time to the cause. All aspects of rapid modernization received attention. Letters from Stalin appeared in virtually every issue of *Komsomol'skaia Pravda*, consistently encouraging the Komsomol to continue the struggle to build Socialism.

Komsomol'skaia Pravda was unquestionably a vital tool for mobilization of effort in the First Five-Year Plan, but its effectiveness in shaping the actual attitudes of its readers remains suspect. Propaganda takes on a different significance in a 'closed' environment.[8] Exposure to a daily flow of propaganda and agitation in this newspaper was a dominant presence in the lives of Soviet citizens; no assessment of a citizen's mentality would be complete without taking this into account. The media was part of a carefully controlled political monopoly, specifically designed to dictate a high degree of uniformity and cooperation. Since there was little or no outside information to compete with it, its potential for influence on human actions and attitudes was greatly magnified.

Komsomol'skaia Pravda thus may be examined as an instrument for controlling the human action. Stalin's programme of rapid social change necessitated cooperation from the masses. Aside from negative methods of coercion, the ruling élite emposed their goals upon the nation through the press. This method had been sanctioned by Lenin when he stated that it was necessary for Communists to 'be able to convince the backward elements'.[9] Stalin further defined leadership as the 'ability to convince the masses that the Party policy is right; ability to issue and act upon slogans that will bring the masses to the Party standpoint'.[10]

Komsomol'skaia Pravda became the lighted torch illuminating the path toward human perfectability in the form of the New Soviet Man, who would by his nature selflessly strive to create a true Communist Society. The success of this medium of communication is evidenced by its sheer volume. In 1939 there were 150 specialized newspapers for young people and children in the Soviet Union, with a circulation of 3 million. At the head were the central Komsomol organs: *Komsomol'skaia Pravda* and *Pioneerskaia Pravda*. Beyond this each republic, territory, and region had its own newspaper for children and youth.[11] This abundance of effort aimed at political indoctrination of the young is a reflection of previous effectiveness.

This study will attempt to demonstrate that the Komsomol evolved within a traditional military orientation, and that Stalin in

1928 successfully appealed to the League with military propaganda in order to enlist its support. The underlying assumption is that Stalin provided Russian youth with a compelling ideology so convincing that it appealed to their still impressionable logic, and so exciting that his goals became theirs with an intensity that neared fanaticism. As a result, this author contends that Komsomol support and participation during the First Five-Year Plan was significant.

Notes

1.   Hans Sebald, *Adolescence: a Social Psychological Analysis.* (New Jersey: Prentice-Hall, 1968) p. 29.
2.   Ibid., p. 29.
3.   Robert V. Daniels (ed.), *The Stalin Revolution* (Lexington, Mass.: D.C. Heath, 1965) p. 1.
4.   Sheila Fitzpatrick, *The Russian Revolution 1917-1932* (Oxford University Press, 1984) p. 110.
5.   Ibid., p. 110.
6.   Alex Inkeles, *Public Opinion in Soviet Russia* (Cambridge, Mass: Harvard University Press, 1967) p. 32.
7.   Ralph Fisher, *Pattern for Soviet Youth* (New York: Columbia University Press, 1959) p. 133.
8.   Inkeles, *Public Opinion*, p. 23.
9.   V. I. Lenin, *Selected Works X* (New York: Progress Publishers, 1942) p. 95.
10. Joseph Stalin, *Leninism* (Leningrad: Cooperative Publishing Society of Foreign Workers in the USSR, 1934) p. 95.
11. Inkeles, *Public Opinion*, pp. 149-50.

1 Background History of the Komsomol: Formation, Consolidation, Disillusionment

The Komsomol struggled with formation and consolidation throughout the first decade of Soviet history. League members experienced relative exuberance during and immediately after conception, followed by inactivity, the surfacing of rival youth groups, and a general disillusionment with the course of the revolution. League participation in the revolution and civil war was extensive, and earned the approval of Lenin. Lenin's attention linked the Komsomol to the Party leadership, and legitimized its strategies. Throughout the NEP years (1917–27) the Komsomol chafed at compromises with capitalism, and tried to break free of ennui and malaise.

Lenin's rhetoric has traditionally served as a touchstone for Soviet leadership since the October Revolution in 1917, when anyone or anything finding favour with Lenin was virtually assured of approval in years to come. It is therefore important to note that Lenin was extremely concerned with the potential of youth to aid in the transformation of Russian society. Lenin himself had been a serious young man, devoting himself to revolutionary study after the execution of his other brother Alexander in 1887. Although Alexander's significance as a role model for the young Lenin is not known, the idea of youthful sacrifice no doubt left a lasting mark. Lenin saw and felt the intense idealism exemplified by young people, and probably believed that more dedicated revolutionaries could not be found. His early writings express his active approval of revolutionary youth, as demonstrated in *V. I. Lenin On Youth,* a collection of articles, speeches, and letters which addressed the problems of Russian youth both before and during the revolution. As early as 1895, while in his prison cell, Lenin drew up the programme of the Russian Social-Democratic Labour Party and put forward demands for universal suffrage for citizens of twenty-one years and over and for a prohibition against the employment of children under the age of fifteen. In August 1903 at the Second Congress of the Social Democratic Party, Lenin sponsored a resolution concerning the party's attitude toward students. This resolution welcomed 'the quickening of revolutionary activity among students and calls on all party organizations to co-operate in every way with the efforts of these students to organize themselves'.[1] In his letters to S. I. Gusev and A. A. Bogdanov he expressed the need to recruit youth 'more widely and bold . . . without fearing them'. Apparently some Social Democrats were hesitant to unleash adolescent energies. Lenin seemed to sense that allowing this distrust and uneasiness to continue would encourage Russian youth to turn their energies against the movement. While in exile, he monitored the student movements on the eve of the Revolution of 1905. In articles in *Iskra*, the illegal Russian Marxist newspaper founded by Lenin in 1900, he urged students to assist the Social Democrats in overthrowing tsarism. All of this suggests that long before 1917, Lenin was concerned with fostering good relations and cooperation between the Russian youth and the older revolutionaries.[2]

Before 1905, the radical youth organizations which existed in the Russian Empire were limited to students, excluding for the most part participation by worker or peasant youth. The 'South Russian Group', originating in 1902 in Rostov-on-Don, was probably the first prototype of the Komsomol. This organization was formed by secondary-school students, newly recruited into the Social Democratic Party, who wished to influence their non-party schoolmates. The chief activity of this group was political education. At its peak it boasted 500 members from such distant places as Baku and Voronezh. Unlike the later Komsomol, the South Russian Group was loosely organized and acted largely on its own initiative. It dissolved in 1904, for no apparent reason other than that its members probably moved up into more important party work.[3]

After the failure of the revolution of 1905, Lenin geared all work of the Bolshevik Party toward the socialist revolution. He stressed the need to educate the masses and to involve the youth in political life, thus allowing them to feel essential to the revolution. In doing this he began to secure the cooperation of young people. Party interest now extended beyond the students, and working youth began joining the party rather than forming separate organizations. In this period, students continued to form separate Social Democratic organizations, especially in Moscow, Riga, and St. Petersburg. However, Lenin was careful not to antagonize these young members of the intelligentsia, especially since he did not have the control over them that he had over those in the Bolshevik Party.[4]

The spirit of battle and struggle which later characterized all Komsomol action was early on instilled and nurtured by Lenin. At the Pirogov Doctors' Congress in 1913, the predominantly bourgeois, professional audience supported a pro-abortion program which advocated saving children the trauma of being brought into a world in which they would be 'maimed' and driven to suicide. Lenin's vehement reaction was that instead of being maimed, the children 'should fight better, more unitedly, consciously and resolutely than we are fighting against the present-day conditions of life which are maiming and ruining our generation'.[5]

There is a lack of information concerning the participation of youth in the February Revolution of 1917. Many radical youth groups did emerge under Provisional Government in the months after February 1917, and poor economic conditions brought these young people to the government with their grievances. Whereas the Provisional Government did not usually respond, the Bolsheviks (unburdened with bureacratic responsibilities) wisely gained youthful support with such proposals as the six-hour work day for minors, free education, paid vacations, and a lowering of the voting age to eighteen.[6]

As a way of addressing these issues, Lenin proposed that the backwardness of Russia was a result of the capitalist exploitation of young people. He announced that the extent to which child labour was being exploited in Russian industry was a direct indication and cause of the plight of the worker. He found this to be true also in the peasant world. In developing his thesis, he drew upon Austrian and German agricultural censuses in a comparative study to show that the number of children and adolescents employed in agriculture was inequitably heavy relative to the total number of persons employed. His study concluded that the exploitation of child labour was greatest on peasant farms in general, and among the middle peasant farms in particular. According to Lenin, the competition of capitalist agriculture compelled the peasant to work his children. The only salvation for the peasant, and for his children, was therefore to join the class struggle of the wage-earners.[7]

These early statements concerning the economic and educational conditions of Russia brought the Bolsheviks tremendous influence over large blocks of young people, especially those in the urban areas, who had genuine proletarian concerns. Following Lenin's lead, the Bolsheviks in 1917 sought to harness the radical energies of the youth, enlist their enthusiasm and support, and at the same time maintain control. This plan required a delicate balance. It is possible that the youth in Russia felt the electricity of revolution in the air and saw opportunity to be at the forefront of one of the greatest events in history. As John Reed said:

> Adventure it was, and one of the most marvelous mankind ever embarked upon, sweeping into history at the head of the toiling masses, and staking everything on their vast and simple desires.[8]

The young people who began following the Bolsheviks, as all youth who crave an adventure or a cause, were acutely aware of the explosive atmosphere. Their desire was to join the struggle to save the world from capitalist exploitation, and they knew they had the power to be the vanguard of such wonderful, larger-than-life endeavour. Lenin made them aware of the necessary tasks at hand and gave them a goal, thus giving them an identity. This endeared him to their hearts. He subsequently withheld formal affiliation with the party from them and dangled it like a carrot on a stick until they demonstrated a willingness to be a subservient arm of the party.

One authority feels that the Komsomol gained an understanding of how it should relate to party authority through examples set by prior youth groups. Socialist youth organizations with varying degrees of success had been in existence since the late 19th century. Their concerns were similar to those of Russian youth in that they were addressing problems of exploitation and inadequate education. The first organized youth group was formed in Belgium in 1886, and its main function was to conduct anti-militaristic propaganda among the young workers being used as strike-breakers. This set a precedent for cooperative communication with the authorities as an alternative to making radical departures from governmental policy, the goal being to avoid antagonizing the authorities in hopes of reaching common ground. Similar groups followed suit in Sweden (1895), Switzerland (1900), Italy (1901), Norway (1902), Spain (1903), and the south of Germany (1904). Their grievances included deplorable working conditions of apprentices and young workers, as well as demands for suffrage. By the time the Bolsheviks were addressing their concerns, Russian youth had learned from the histories of these previous organizations that working within the party was the best way to achieve success, especially considering that the Provisional Government had already snubbed them. Similarly, the Bolshevik Party had realized the importance of addressing the problems of youth, especially as the young people became more organized.[9]

In Russia, Petrograd became an early centre of organized youthful activity. In May 1917, a coalition of factory youths designated themselves 'Labour and Light' and welcomed into their ranks Mensheviks, Bolsheviks, Socialist Revolutionaries, anarchists, and others. P.Shevtsov was the leader of this group, whose main objective was to minimize the cultural and political differences within the group in order to achieve solidarity. However, the moderate nature of 'Labour and Light' was not in keeping with the volatile political currents surging around it. The notion of compromise was adverse to Bolshevik ideology, and party members were determined to undermine the group. Young Bolsheviks infiltrated 'Labour and Light' and raised protests, charging it with 'social and political unawareness'. In June, the Bolsheviks set up a rival city-wide youth group under the name of 'Socialist League of Working Youth', led by the young Bolshevik Vasili Alekseev.[10]

On 20 August, an all-city conference of working youth dissolved 'Labour and Light' and endorsed the 'Socialist League of Working Youth of Petrograd'.[11] The element of party control is a key point in Western historical analysis of Russian youth leagues. Soviet historians claim that the formation of the 'Socialist League of Working Youth of Petrograd' was spontaneous and independent from party control. Although spontaneity may have been present, this author believes it is more likely that the Socialist youth realized the political advantage of following Bolshevik guidance. Similarly, the Bolsheviks welcomed the opportunity to bring the youth organization into the fold. The very nature of young people makes them rankle at the thought of being controlled by authority figures, unless the goals of the two groups are consonant. If the Bolsheviks had come on too strong, the youth may have resisted involvement and affiliation.

In the summer of 1917, the Bolsheviks began debating the issue of setting up a youth subsidiary of the party. While some members favored a youth organization directly under the control of the party, others (such as Lenin's wife, Krupskaya) favored a mass proletarian organization really run by the young people themselves. She declared that 'friendly relations with young people are essential, otherwise youth will move away from us'. The Sixth Party Congress, in August of 1917, passed a resolution 'On Youth Leagues' which declared that 'the Party of the proletariat . . . realizes the tremendous significance which working youth has for the working class movement as a whole', and advertised itself as a champion of youth's 'active participation in the economic and political struggle of the working class'. No other party at this time had issued a direct appeal to the youth.[12]

Soviet and western historians differ in their interpretations of the Sixth Party Congress. The western view suggests that it was at this congress that the Bolsheviks began exerting influence and control over the youth in order to keep them in line with party goals. Soviet accounts state that the party, never having neglected the vast strength and revolutionary possibilities of the youth, turned its attention at the Sixth Party Congress to the creation of an official, party-affiliated Russian youth organization. Soviet historians deny the existence of any 'Bolshevik dictatorship' over the youth, and have argued against such interpretations by western historians.[13]

Within a week after seizure of power in November 1917, the Bolshevik government addressed specific problems which concerned youth: it established limits on working hours and on employment conditions for adolescents, enfranchised eighteen- and nineteen-year-old workers, and granted them tuition-free entry into the universities.[14] This suggests that Lenin viewed the youth as a powerful force that should receive attention and consideration.

The Communist party officially established the Komsomol in August 1918. The Komsomol held its first three formal congresses during the years 1918–20. The agendas included clarification of demands to the party, and examination of two perpetual problems: how to 'inculcate discipline in youth without eliminating initiative', and what 'roles the Komsomol would perform in the various spheres of Soviet life'.[15]

At the first Komsomol Congress, 194 representatives of various worker and peasant youth groups throughout the country were present as voting delegates. They represented 120 youth groups with a total of 22 100 members. Of these 88 were Communist party members, 38 were party sympathizers, and 45 were non-party. The delegates agreed upon the following: '1. the League is solidary with the Russian Communist Party (Bolsheviks), and 2. the League is an independent organization,'[16] Apparently the two were deemed compatible. At this early congress of 1918, a dispute arose over whether or not to call the League Communist, the concern being how inclusive this would render membership. There was no question of loyalty to Communism. Lazar Shatskin, a presiding officer, arrived at the name 'Communist League of Youth', the first Russian syllables of which formed the name Komsomol. The organization would not be limited to Communist youth, but would also include uncommitted worker and peasant youth. This First Congress also established the administrative skeleton of the group and clearly stated that the All-Russian Congress of the Bolshevik Party was to be the supreme authority. Lenin provided for the financial needs of the organization by an informal order to Iakov M. Sverdlov, chairman of the Central Executive Committee of the Party.[17]

The Komsomol received official recognition from the Bolshevik party at the Eighth Party Congress, 18-23 March 1919. Western historians claim that by the time the Second Komsomol Congress met on October of 1919, the members of the Komsomol were not only collectively, but also individually subject to party control. Evidence to support this view is cited with reference to the Third Komsomol Congress, which enacted a new program and regulations, stressing that any suggestion of decentralization was viewed as a threat to party control and hence considered an anti-party action.[18]

Lenin knew that simply to bring the youth into the revolution, while at the same time keeping them on short rein, would not preserve their loyalty. He had as early as 1903 agreed with an editorial in the newspaper *Student* which recognized that 'revolutionary sentiment alone cannot bring about ideological unity among the students . . . '. He attacked the Social Revolutionaries for their view on 'non-partisanship', favouring instead the loyalty to a 'definite political spirit' for the sake of the revolution.[19] Lenin had thus set a precedent for the Komsomol which instructed that youth should not only be committed to the party, but that they should also tolerate no political divisions. The Komsomol, with party urging, took this view to heart and in 1918 declared itself the only true communist youth organization. To disrupt an established rival, the Boy Scouts, some members of the Bolshevik party attempted to lure part of the Boy Scouts over to a newly inspired group, the 'Young Communists'. The Komsomol would tolerate neither group, suggesting that the principal defect of the Young Communists was that their political education was merely verbal. The Komsomol voted to liquidate them in August 1919, and embarked upon one of its first propaganda campaigns. The Scout organizations in all towns were charged with 'leaning in the direction of the White Guards'. Scout discipline was charged with being too militaristic.[20]

During the civil war years, Lenin referred to the Komsomolites as 'Great Initiators', and praised them for their heroic struggle. Field camps under Lenin's guidance sheltered young people who selflessly and enthusiastically increased the amount of labour available for economic and industrial recovery following the devastation of civil war. This was especially true in the area of pig iron production, which had fallen drastically from pre-revolutionary levels, and benefited greatly from Komsomol 'shock troops' which volunteered for labour. In his article 'Great Initiators', Lenin announced that true Communism had begun with their efforts.[21] League participation in the military during the civil war was extensive, and will be covered in Chapter-2.

The NEP, enacted by Lenin in 1921, had a dispiriting effect on the morale of the Komsomol, as it did on many Bolsheviks. Most of the Komsomol membership had enthusiastically supported War Communism measures during the civil war, and subsequently resented the contrasting compromises of NEP. Bukharin best described the psychological atmosphere during these years of relaxed attitudes toward capitalism. He said the NEP

> . . . has not set before youth any rigorous, colorful, sharply defined, militant, heroic task. In the period of the civil war there stood before youth a colossal task of unprecedented beauty. It captivated them; their relations to it were usually clear and

obvious: they had to kill the common enemy, world capital-
ism . . . so there has come with the shift of the New Economic
Policy a sort of demoralization, a sort of spiritual crisis among
Communist Youth . . . [22]

Although NEP was deemed necessary, the party realized that
compromise and lack of purpose was repulsive to the largest
reservoir of constructive energy in the Soviet Union. No doubt this
caused the leadership a degree of anxiety, although they had
plenty to worry about other than a pack of frustrated adolescents.

The disillusionment and relative inactivity of the Komsomol
during NEP was reflected in the absence of any real surge in
membership. Membership jumped from 22 000 in 1918 to 400 000
in 1920 due to Bolshevik fortunes in the civil war. Although
membership continued to grow incrementally through NEP, this
was probably more an indication of population growth that of
actual interest. The entire membership did increase by 300 000
during NEP, but another big jump did not occur until 1928, when
it rose from 700 000 to 2 000 000. The NEP years are thus
considered ones of a 'levelling off' of interest.[23]

During the NEP years, the government embarked upon a programme of religious persecution. In 1925 a society of the 'Militant
Godless' was formed among Communist Youth. The Militant
Godless converted many churches into anti-religious museums,
published atheist magazines, and painted crude posters depicting
Christ as an evil merchant. This antagonized many religious
people in the Soviet Union. In attempting to set the minor reli-
gions against the Russian Orthodox Church, the government
briefly allowed such groups as the Baptists to thrive and conduct
Sunday schools. A 'Christomol' society of Christian youth was
formed which rivalled the Komsomol in membership.[24] While
caught up in the anti-religious campaign, many Komsomolites
found themselves waging war with their own families. It may have
seemed that the real revolution against capitalism had been side-
tracked.

The extent of disillusionment cited by Bukharin and others
suggests that the Komsomol felt that all it had worked and fought
for in the revolution was being lost. League members had been
considered the dynamic element in the drive to create a new
socialist society, and were charged with inculcating in themselves
the qualities of the 'New Communist Man'. Unable to accept

bourgeois retreats from this ideal, the members of the Komsomol, under the guidance of Shatskin, endeavoured to fortify themselves ideologically against the surrounding forces of capitalism. The League embarked on numerous campaigns against alcoholism and moral decadence as if to remain pure amidst abundant evil.[25] A sort of siege mentality came to dominate the organization, as the members turned their efforts inward to reinforce discipline, character, and moral excellence. Many of the Komsomolites had been too young to fight in the real revolution and civil war battles for Communism, and were eager for action. By not providing an outlet for that action, the party may have come dangerously close to losing the support of the Komsomol, which was growing increasingly restless, angry, and bored.

Bukharin urged the Komsomol to develop its spirit of competition in sports, hoping to distract it from the political stagnation of NEP. Although for much of the NEP period Bukharin served as the party's liaison with the Komsomol, and as spokesman on youth, he was resented by those in the League. Sheila Fitzpatrick attributes his lack of rapport to a statement he made describing the typical Komsomol leader as 'an ignorant, manipulative little apparatchik'.[26]

By the end of NEP, the Komsomol had become organized and experienced, as following chapters will show, in military affairs, education drives, and the ability to motivate its membership through propaganda. On the down side, the League was disenchanted with the party leadership, and felt the revolution had been betrayed. The Komsomol needed someone to give it a chance to wage war against all elements which threatened to erode the foundations of socialism. Stalin was the man.

Notes

1. Robert H. McNeal (ed.) *Resolutions and Decisions of the Communist Party of the Soviet Union, vol. I* (University of Toronto Press, 1974) p. 54.
2. V. I. Lenin, *Lenin On Youth* (Moscow: Progress Publishers, 1980) p. 180.
3. Ralph Fisher, *Pattern for Soviet Youth* (New York: Columbia University Press, 1959) p. 3.
4. Ibid., p. 4.
5. Lenin, *Lenin On Youth*, pp. 31–3.
6. Fisher, *Soviet Youth*, p. 5.

7.   Lenin, *Lenin On Youth*, pp. 36–7.
8.   John Reed, *Ten Days that Shook the World* (New York: Signet Books, 1967) p. 19.
9.   Richard Cornell, *Youth and Communism* (New York: Walker & Co., 1965) p. 13.
10. Fisher, *Soviet Youth*, pp. 6–7. For the Soviet account, see E. V. Danilenko, 'Questions of Party Control Over Komsomol According to American Historians', *Vestnik Leningradskogo Universiteta*, 1970, no. 7, p. 40.
11. Sidney I. Ploss, 'Forty Years of the Komsomol', The *Soviet Union*, 1978, no. 2, p. 9.
12. Ibid., p. 9.
13. Danilenko, 'Questions of Party Control', p. 43.
14. Ploss, 'Forty Years', p. 9.
15. Fisher, *Soviet Youth*, p. 43.
16. Ibid., pp, 9–10.
17. Ibid., p. 12.
18. Ibid., p. 13. For the Soviet view see Danilenko, 'Questions of Party Control', p. 44.
19. Lenin, *Lenin On Youth, pp. 87_95.*
20. *Fisher, Soviet Youth*, p. 19.
21. *Komsomol'skaia Pravda*, 17 Nov. 1928, p. 6.
22. Fisher, *Soviet Youth*, p. 80.
23. Ellsworth Raymond, *The Soviet State* (New York: Walker & Co., 1978) p. 279.
24. Ibid., p. 82.
25. Fisher, *Soviet Youth*, p. 300.
26. Sheila Fitzpatrick (ed.), *Cultural Revolution in Russia, 1928–1931* (Indiana University Press, 1978) p. 16.

2 From Militarization to Industrialization

In 1927 Komsomolites were steeped in military discipline, and responded eagerly to Stalin's appeal for 'soldiers' in the drive for rapid modernization. Some older members had combat experience from participation in the revolution as well as the civil war. The League had thus far been instrumental in organizing political education groups within the armed forces, and had been conspicuously present on the battle fronts. So intense was Komsomol attention to national defense that by the beginning of the First Five-Year Plan military jargon dominated its rhetoric and action. Stalin took advantage of this fighting tradition and urged the Komsomol to wage full-scale war on any form of opposition to his goals. Every aspect of the First Five-Year Plan became a battle front.

In the days prior to the October Revolution, young Bolsheviks actively trained for the coming insurrection by carrying out military drills. Students and young workers poured into Petrograd from Moscow, Odessa, Kiev, and Rostov-on-Don to join in the adventure, the bulk of these young men serving in detachments of the Red Guard.[1] On the night of 25 October, over 5000 youth took part in the armed takeover of Petrograd. Trotsky had assigned them the task of seizing a majority of key points, such as train depots and telegraph stations.[2]

At the time of the Bolshevik Revolution, Lenin and the Bolshevik Party did not have a definite plan for the construction of an army. Although the notion of an official standing army was being debated, Lenin had long since made one thing clear: 'The need for a revolutionary army derives from the fact that great historical issues can be resolved only by force.'[3] This view was not lost on Bolshevik youth, and in fact carried over as a golden rule in the Komsomol. Lenin's ideas for the construction of an effective military system included a general modification of all provincial districts, though it was not ascertained just how this was to be done, nor who was to do it. Equally crucial was the need to build a positive attitude among the masses (especially those of fighting age) which would foster support for the party. After becoming an official organization in 1918, the Komsomol focused its efforts on generating this support. League members were excited by the prospect of serving as real soldiers in the revolution, and were determined to make loyalty to the cause infectious. Komsomolites entered the Red Guard as a special brigade in February of 1918, and declared their unified allegiance to the party.[4]

The political commissar provided one of the earliest means of ensuring correct political attitudes within the army itself. It was Alexander Kerensky, not the Bolsheviks, who established this office, in order to cut down on massive desertions from the front during World War I. The Bolshevik Party first used the commissar in October 1917, when the Military Revolutionary Committee dispatched them into the Petrograd garrison to overthrow the Provisional Government. It was not an early requirement that the political commissars be Bolsheviks, only revolutionaries. On 8 April 1918, the All-Russian Bureau of Military Commissars was placed under the chairmanship of K. K. Yurenev.[5]

Commissars were as responsible for the actions of the Red Army soldiers as were the commanders. Trotsky was particulary notorious for court-martialling and shooting commissars if their troops behaved inappropriately. Order no. 337 of the *Revvoensovet* (revolutionary soviet) on 15 December 1918 declared that political organs were formed on all fronts, in all divisions. That same month 6309 military commissars were at work among the troops.[6]

At its Eighth Congress in March 1919, the party appealed to the League to take the initiative in filling the role of political commissar. Not unexpectedly, the youth responded positively and focused their attention on national defence, replenishment of personnel in the Red Army, and adequate training and political education for commanders. As political commissars, Komsomolites strove to be examples of spirit, discipline, and forthrightness. The actual work of the commissar included formation of party cells and lectures, and the construction of cultural clubs and reading rooms. By July 1919, virtually every battle front in the civil war had a commissar contingent of which 39 to 45 per cent were Komsomol youths of 23 years of age or younger.[7]

Until the end of 1918 there was no compulsory military conscription. Thus, the first part of the civil war was fought by a Red Army composed entirely of volunteer workers, peasants, and men left over from the Tsarist army and navy. On 22 April 1918 military training became compulsory for 'workers and those peasants who do not exploit the labor of others'.[8] Women could also volunteer, although it is not clear how many actually did. When universal conscription became law on 29 May 1918, the Komsomol was immediately directed to organize mobilizations. Throughout the war it repeatedly carried out this task under orders from the party. Between 1918 and 1920 Komsomol mobilizations contributed over ten thousand men to the Red Army.[9] Admiral Alexander V. Kolchak's menace in the East caused the first 'all-Russian' (nation-wide) Komsomol mobilization on 19 May 1919, and brought 3000 young people into the armed forces. The League was responsible for training its own men. Although most Komsomolites went into regular Red Army units where they served as commissars and agitators as well as soldiers in combat, many formed special outfits such as bicycle teams and ski patrols in the Urals.[10] In the summer of 1918 the Moscow Alliance of Working Youth sent 300 members to the Eastern front, one of the more troublesome spots at the time due to Kolchak's incursions as well as aggression from the Czech Legion and the Japanese. By 1919 10 per cent of the troops on that front were Komsomolites.[11]

With the establishment of military conscription, the First Komsomol Congress in October 1918 formally committed the League to aid in the armed defence of the regime and to encourage military training among youth.[12] The League simply continued its practice of mass mobilizations which had previously been voluntary. By the time of the Second Congress in October 1919, General A. I. Denikin's Volunteers were little more than 200 miles from Moscow, and Iudenich was nearing Petrograd. Needless to say, the Bolsheviks were becoming anxious, and needed a turn of events. Trotsky spoke out on behalf of the Red Army, and cited the army's extensive dependence on the Komsomol to fill such positions as cavalry, ski detachments, reconnaisance, and liaison. In effect, the military looked to the Youth League to provide the additional manpower and enthusiasm necessary to win the war. The Komsomol responded with large mobilizations of young men within the year, specifically in provinces bordering on battle zones: Kaluga, Tula, Riazan, Orel, Tambov, and Voronezh. The age limit was sixteen and over. These drives resulted in a surge of 40 000 new recruits to the fronts. In addition, the League was now directed to take over military training, not just for its own members, but for all new conscripts.[13]

There was a great deal of heroism on the part of Komsomolites during the civil war. Young men of fifteen and sixteen years of age advanced rapidly to command positions. Their exploits were legendary, and some became immortalized in the classic civil war novel, *How the Steel Was Tempered*, by Nikolai Ostrovsky. Ostrovsky himself was critically wounded on the battlefront, and survived to write about the courage and determination of the Komsomol during that war. His book was a great inspiration to youth in the 1920s and 1930s who longed to have a chance to fight their own war.[14]

Albert Lapin, aged 17, was one of these youthful civil war heroes. Lapin went to the Eastern front and performed so effectively that he became the substitute commander of a 30-man rifle division. One of his comrades, Arcady Golikov, became a troop commander at age 16, went on to the officers school in Moscow at eighteen, and afterwards commanded troops as a marshal in the Red Army. I. Krylov finished his infantry machine-gun course at age seventeen, and became the commander of battalions on the Southern, Caucasian, and Far Eastern fronts.[15]

In March 1919 a committee of the Eighth Party Congress reached a decision concerning formal admission to commander's courses for the Red Army. The Central Committee expressed concern that workers and peasants should have more opportunities to receive military commissions. The Komsomol seized this opportunity to present its prime candidates of worker and peasant background.[16] The Central Committee obligingly admitted 12 Komsomolites into the Petrograd commanders' course in May 1919. Thus encouraged, the League rapidly mobilized its membership to apply for the commanders' course in every province. Over 2000 Komsomolites soon became students in military academies throughout the country. Within the year, 70 per cent of all men in Siberian military academies were Komsomolites. Women in the Komsomol were encouraged to receive special training and to form nurses corps.[17]

By the end of the civil war, the reputation of the military prowess of the Communist Youth League was securely intact, as was its foothold in military affairs. Over one-third of all Komsomol members had served in the Red Army, which included over 7000, 500 youthful soldiers, commanders, and political workers. These young people had acquitted themselves bravely, perhaps turning the tide of the war. Komsomolites accounted for 5000, 215 young soldiers who were awarded the Order of the Red Banner, a token of supreme sacrifice to the Soviet regime.[18]

With the onset of NEP, the Komsomol found itself with no war to fight, but most members wished to continue the focus on military preparedness. Since the League had been charged with military training, it responded to appeals from its younger members and initiated combat-oriented sports for pre-military age youngsters. Beginning with organized sport in 1920, the Komsomol created a broad network of military-sports clubs which provided another environment for propagating political and cultural education outside the regular army.[19] These clubs stressed combat readiness, and put their members through rigorous exercises in camoflage, riflery, and foxhole-digging. The payoff was rapid advancement to non-commissioned officer status upon reaching conscription age.[20]

The Komsomol did not neglect the Red Navy in its military involvements. After the devastation of the civil war, it took part in the restoration of ships and submarine, along with the construction of new shipbuilding centres located primarily in the vicinity of Petrograd. In the absence of actual opportunities for armed combat, Komsomolites threw themselves into these tasks with a vengeance, for which they were rewarded: between 1922 and 1924, more than 8000 League members were accepted into the Naval Academy in Petrograd.[21]

For the remainder of the NEP years, the Komsomol focused on military training in the form of sports clubs. An official military and sport commission was created in the League in 1926, and coordinated work on military propaganda. Despite these efforts, the lack of a real war combined with the obvious compromises of NEP, dampened the spirit of the Komsomol. The leadership struggled to keep members out of the Vodka and involved in technical training, riflery, and intelligence work.[22] Though at times it seemed the Vodka was winning out, this military image of the Komsomol was one of the few endeavours which staved off total apathy.

In 1927, all sports clubs and para-military exercises united into one mass society which was officially labelled Osoaviakhim. Its membership began at a nation-wide total of 2 million, mostly Komsomol, and increased steadily, reaching twelve million by the end of the First Five-Year Plan. Renamed DOSAAF (Volunteer Society to Aid the Army, Air Force, and Naval Fleet) after World War II, the Osoaviakhim was a militia, home guard, and civil defence rolled up into one. The first amateur flying club in the USSR was an early product of this organization, as was the world's first paratroop training programme. Osoaviakhim units were the only place a young man could own and operate a ham radio set. By 1931, the Komsomol had through Osoaviakhim created the Ready for Labour and Defence (GTO) Test, which was a series of seven semi-militarized decathlons. This series included sprinting, cross-country running, swimming, gymnastics, skiing or bike riding, hand grenade throwing, map reading, and rifle shooting. The swimming sometimes was done while carrying a weapon, and the shooting could be from horseback or during the cross-country run.[23]

As a result of this intense focus on military training and orientation throughout the NEP, by 1927 the Komsomol was not only a very organized military group, but a very ambitious and frustrated one. Its membership occupied a large portion of the command positions within the Red Army and Red Navy, as well as the political commissar slots. Komsomolites were trained to fight and eager to do so. Their heroes were their predecessors in the civil war. What they lacked was a war of their own, a chance to go to battle and prove themselves. This they wanted desperately, and Stalin was aware of the fact. Before the year was out, he threw the country into a war crisis mentality to set the stage for crash industrialization and collectivization. Stalin's war crisis was made more plausible when difficulties with Great Britian and the National Kuomintang in China conveniently renewed the threat of captialist intervention.[24]

Having aroused a sense of urgency, Stalin used this mind-set to begin making demands on the population. He chose the Komsomol to set the wheels in motion for the First Five-Year Plan. His first step was to unleash them on his enemies, beginning with the Trotskyite Opposition. The Eighth Komsomol Congress of 1928 detailed the struggle against enemies of the people. Trotskyists were those who wanted a 'defensive' reserve militia rather than an offensive standing army. The Komsomol membership was dominated by an offensive frame of mind. Additional villains included various types of 'class enemies' whom Bukharin identified for the League as kulaks (who had reportedly killed several Komsomolites), and religious organizations such as the Baptist youth (Baptomol) and Christian youth (Khristomol).[25]

Speaking on the last day of the Eighth Komsomal Congress,

Stalin warned that a few years of peace had caused the people to forget the enemy. He called for more militancy and vigilance. The task of 'socialist construction' was thus formally assigned to the Komsomol with defininte military overtones. Chaplin, the Chairman of the League, appealed to the membership to initiate a massive volunteer programme to draw millions of young people into the push for production. The tone of this entire Congress harkened back to the civil war when the youth had been called upon to voluntarily save Russia. At last another glorious mission seemed to be at hand. The Komsomol rapidly formed 'shock work battalions' which accomplished phenomenal feats on the 'industrial front'.[26]

The commitment of the Komsomol to rapid industrialization fitted neatly into Stalin's imagery of an impending war. Sheila Fitzpatrick suggests the situation 'symbolized a return to the spirit of civil war and war Communism and a repudiation of the unheroic compromises of NEP'.[27] Military propaganda was intensified in *Komsomol'skaia Pravda*, which introduced combat jargon into virtually every headline in 1928. All group action on the part of the Komsomol was labelled in military terms, such as 'light cavalry', 'brigades', and every task was a 'front'. Collectivization at some points necessitated 'guerilla warfare'. Komsomolites who had served in the Red Army brought military jargon into everyday life. The army tunic and boots were worn by those in civilian posts as well as those too young to enlist. Military uniforms became a status symbol for upward-striving Komsomol and party members in the 1920s and 1930s.[28]

No other group rivalled the Komsomol in its efforts to propagandize the industrial drive in order to elicit support from its constituency. The League not only urged its membership to work, it publicized accomplishments, arranged competitions, and chastised those who did not exhibit proper levels of enthusiasm. In addition to calling on youth for volunteer work, *Komsomol'skaia Pravda* also urged a renewed commitment to the Red Army. This was also in accordance with rapid industrialization, since the army was a large organized source of labour.

The intensity of the drive for rapid industrialization has been accurately described by Adam Ulam:

Every Soviet producer . . . would become a soldier in the war to attain the goal prescribed from above. Fulfillment or nonfulfillment of quotas would become equivalent to soldierly behavior and desertion under fire. Stalinism came to mean many things, but chief among them was this relentless struggle to produce, to sacrifice everything but the dictator's personal power at the altar of industrialization. . . . One's daily work became a test of one's loyalty.[29]

As in the case of collectivization, the aura surrounding rapid industrialization was one of fighting, of battles, of sacrifice. For the Komsomol, this was a welcome relief from NEP.

At giant industrial complexes such as Dneprostroi, Mangi-tostroi, Kusnetskstroi, and Traktorstroi, the trade unions tried to create model working and living conditions for the workers. The party attempted to foster a climate of shared communal goods, and encouraged workers with incentives and technical training. Special attention was given to those groups which had been discriminated against in the past: women, young workers, and nationalist minorities. All of this was done in the spirit of righting previous wrongs. Unfortunately, as policies changed during the First Five-Year Plan and production quotas received more priority than working conditions, resistance arose among the work force.[30] It was in the struggle against this resistance that the party again turned to the Komsomol.

On 28 May 1928, a 'Letter from Stalin' appeared in *Komsomol'-skaia Pravda*. In this letter Stalin wished the Komsomol success on every 'front', and urged them to retain their courage in the face of inevitable opposition. They were asked to continue fighting for Communism and its ideals, and to be diligent in routing out old remnants of bureacracy and corruption. He appealed to them to maintain a solid, united front until victory was achieved. Stalin charged the youth with the bulk of the struggle to build Socialism, and stated that he knew they would never let him down.[31] This letter was repeated in different forms many times; the tone was always the same: Stalin wanted the Komsomol to know that he approved of them and counted on them.

Stalin's words received no debate in the League. The Eighth Komsomol Congress was devoted almost entirely to the task of 'Socialist Construction', especially in heavy industry. Chaplin stressed the need for vast expansion of the shock-group movement:

We will assign tasks, we will demand the fulfillment of League obligations; otherwise we will not be a solidary Bolshevik Communist organization. Therefore the Komsomolite must combine both voluntariness and obligatory tasks, placing the main stress on the development of inititative and voluntariness . . .[32]

The object of shock-group movements was not to set the youth apart from the older workers, but to draw them 'into the general current of the constructive work of the proletariat'.[33] Unfortunately, the exuberance of the Komsomolites irritated the older workers, and the young people began to feel ostracized and somewhat disillusioned. This took time however, since youth are by nature persistent and resilient.

One outgrowth of the shock-group movement was the Subbotnik, which was voluntary work on Saturdays or holidays. This concept was in keeping with the selfless revolutionary zeal of many League members, and even after it ceased to be so, *Komsomol'skaia Pravda* shamed individuals into perpetuating their enthusiasm. Each week the paper ran extensive coverage on as many Subbotniks as possible throughout the country. Examples included 5000 students who on 29 October 1928 spent the day helping three different manufacturers with cleaning and repairs.[34] Many voluntary work days were spent cleaning tools and instruments in various factories and in gathering fuel for furnaces: These projects were great social gatherings for the youth, and an excellent chance for them to put their idealism to practical use.[35]

A resolution of the Eighth Komsomol Congress introduced competition into League propaganda. Komsomolites were ordered to organize production contests between individual young workers, groups of workers of similar skill, between shops in the same factory, and between factories.[36] This 'socialist competition' also took hold in the Subbotnik movement. *Komsomol'skaia Pravda* took great pains to print production outputs for different groups side by side on the front page.[37] The more difficult the task, the more attention lavished upon it. For example, when Komsomolites worked their Subbotniks without pay, striving only to move a factory closer to meeting its quota, they received a great deal of praise and publicity.

In the factory environment, a police function was one of the most important activities of the League. As conditions for the workers grew worse due to the shifting of emphasis to meeting quotas, bad attitudes threatened to affect production. Bukharin suggested that special groups of Komsomolites go 'under cover' and walk through stores, institutions, and commissariats to act like normal customers or petitioners to see what kind of treatment they received. These unofficial inspection teams called themselves 'light cavalry', just as they did on collectivization drives. The Komsomol supplemented regular party agencies in this work, and were only too happy to do so.[38] Histories of individual Komsomol organizations place great emphasis on this watchdog function during the First Five-Year Plan.[39]

On 15 November 1928, *Komsomol'skaia Pravda* printed a front page story describing how the Baimanskogo regional Komsomol conducted a thorough checkup of factories in the area to verify that machines and tools were kept clean, that attitudes of the masters toward working youth were congenial, and that production was up to par. This event was initiated by the editorial staff of *Komsomol'skaia Pravda*.[40] Apparently this form of propaganda served a two-fold function: to announce that the League was actively promoting increased production, and to publicize any bad attitudes among factory management towards Stalin or the youth. These check-ups were also to serve as examples to all workers of the proper diligence displayed by the 'New Soviet Man'.

By the end of 1929, Stalin stated in an article in *Pravda* that he felt there had been a marked change in labour productivity. This change consisted of an expansion of 'creative initiative' and intense 'labour enthusiasm'. He believed this achievement was the result of 3 factors:

(a) the fight – by means of self-criticism – against bureacracy, which shackles the labour initiative and labour productivity of the masses;

(b) the fight – by means of socialist emulation – against the labour shirkers and disrupters of proletarian labour discipline; and finally

(c) the fight – by the introduction of the uninterrupted work week (days of rest were rotated, so the factory never shut down) – against routine and inertia in industry.[41]

The rise and maintenance of labour enthusiasm was clearly considered by Stalin to be the most significant factor in the First

Five-Year Plan. He highly valued the one organization which made optimism and enthusiasm for his goals its top priority. If he had been speaking to a more mature, seasoned audience, his rhetoric might have been less loaded with militaristic catch words. But he was speaking to zealous youth, and was careful to tell them what they wanted to hear.

Throughout the First Five-Year Plan, the Komsomol continually provided a large reservoir of manpower for extraordinarily demanding undertakings. This was evidenced by the Stalingrad tractor factory, the Dnepropetrovsk electric power combine, construction of factories and lumber camps in the Urals and Siberia, the coal mines of the Donbas, and the Moscow subway.[42] The climax of Komsomol participation came with the construction of Komsomolsk-on-Amur. In 1930, Komsomol members from all parts of the Soviet Union joined in a massive effort to build an entire town. This town was to function as an industrial centre in the Khabarovsk region. Work on this project continued throughout the 1930s, and remains a symbol of Komsomol devotion to the building of socialism, and an inspiration to Komsomol members.[43] All of this effort was rewarded by the party. *Komsomol'skaia Pravda* received the Order of the Red Banner in 1931.[44]

In many ways, the Soviet Union during the First Five-Year Plan did resemble a nation at war, a very justified and noble war, at least in theory. Arthur Koestler, at one time a devoted Communist, 'fell in love with the First Five-Year Plan', and recounted his feelings prior to actually visiting Russia:

> On one-sixth of our sick planet, the most gigantic construction effort of all times had begun; there Utopia was being built in steel and concrete . . . Russia had undertaken the greatest engineering experiment in history – at a time when the remaining five-sixths of the world were visibly falling to pieces. Marxist theory and Soviet practice were the admirable and ultimate fulfillment of the nineteenth century's ideal of Progress, to which I owed allegiance. The greatest electric power dam in the world must surely bring the greatest happiness to the greatest number.[45]

After arriving in Russia, Koestler found that the Komsomol, who shared his lofty ideas, were truely at war with the forces of reality:

. . . Let us not deceive ourselves: this writer did not stand up very well to the test of the first few days. . . . He had visualized the Soviet Union as a kind of gigantic Manhattan with enormous buildings sprouting from the earth like mushrooms after rain, with rivers queing up before power stations, mountains being tossed into the air by faith, and people breathlessly racing, as in an accelerated film to fulfill the plan. . . . Only slowly does the newcomer learn to think in contradictions; to distinguish, underneath a chaotic surface, the shape of things to come; to realize that in Sovietland the present is a fiction, a quivering membrane stretched between the past and the future . . . [46]

If Koestler's perceptions were accurate, why then did the Komsomol continue to serve Stalin with such devotion? Quite simply, it would appear that Stalin appealed to their logic. Adolescents tend to be very egocentric. By the age of 14, many of them have achieved some proficiency in logical analysis; as a result their newfound logic is glorious and very personal. It is guarded defensively and thought to be infallible. The members of the Komsomol had by 1928 become convinced that they were the saviors of the revolution, reinforced by their history of service in the revolution and civil war, and validated by Stalin, who gave them the authority to act on their dreams.

Notes

1. *Armiia i Komsomol*, 'Molodaia Gvardiia' (Moscow: Progress Publisher, 1983) p. 22.
2. Ibid., p. 10.
3. Michael J. Deane, *Political Control of the Soviet Armed Forces* (New York: Crane, Russak, 1977) p. 4.
4. *Armiia i Komsomol*, p. 22.
5. Deane, *Political Control*, p. 15.
6. Ibid., pp. 16–17.
7. *Armiia i Komsomol*, p. 31.
8. Ralph Fisher, *Pattern for Soviet Youth* (New York: Columbia University Press, 1959) p. 323.
9. *Armiia i Komsomol*, p. 11.
10. Fisher, *Soviet Youth*, p. 48.
11. *Armiia i Komsomol*, p. 24.

12.   Fisher, *Soviet Youth*, p. 47.
13.   Ibid., pp. 48–9.
14.   Nicholia Ostrovsky, *How the Steel Was Tempered* (Moscow: Progress Publishers, 1979). Ostrovsky lived from 1904 to 1936. He suffered severe wounds during the Civil War which later incapacitated him. His novel is based on Komsomol exploits during the early years of Soviet rule.
15.   *Armiia i Komsomol*, p. 30.
16.   Ibid., p. 22.
17.   Ibid., p. 26.
18.   Ibid., p. 38. The Order of the Red Banner, a symbol of honour awarded for extraordinary acts of sacrifice, was first presented on 16 September 1918.
19.   Ellsworth Raymond, *The Soviet State* (New York: Walker & Co., 1978) pp. 283–4.
20.   Ibid., pp. 283–4.
21.   *Armiia i Komsomol*, p. 41.
22.   Raymond, *Soviet State*, p. 284.
23.   Ibid., p. 284.
24.   Sheila Fitzpatrick, *The Russian Revolution, 1917–1932* (Oxford University Press, 1984) p. 110.
25.   Fisher, *Soviet Youth*, p. 143.
26.   Ibid., p. 157.
27.   Fitzpatrick, *Russian Revolution*, p. 110.
28.   Ibid., p. 64.
29.   Adam Ulam, *Stalin: the Man and His Era* (New York: The Viking Press, 1973) p. 293.
30.   Anne D. Rassweiler, 'Soviet Labour Policy in the First Five-Year Plan: the Dneprostroi Experience', *Slavic Review*, 1983, no. 2, p. 231.
31.   *Komsomol'skaia Pravda*, 26 May 1928, p. 1.
32.   Fisher, *Soviet Youth*, p. 157.
33.   Ibid., p. 157.
34.   *Komsomol'skaia Pravda*, 21 Oct. 1928, p. 4.
35.   *Pravda*, 28 Oct. 1928, p. 4.
36.   Fisher, *Soviet Youth*, p. 161.
37.   *Komsomol'skaia Pravda*, 15 Nov. 1928, p. 4.
38.   Fisher, *Soviet Youth*, p. 158.
39.   *Komsomol'skaia Pravda*, 15 Nov. 1928, p. 4.
40.   Ibid., p. 4.
41.   Joseph Stalin, *Selected Writings* (New York: Progress Publishers, 1942) p. 135.
42.   Richard Cornell, *Youth and Communism* (New York: Walker & Co., 1965) p. 49.
43.   *The Komsomol: Questions and Answers* (Moscow: International Publishers, 1980) p. 165.
44.   Ibid., pp. 125–6.
45.   Arthur Koestler, *Arrow in the Blue* (New York: Macmillan, 1952) pp. 278–9.
46.   Arthur Koestler, *The Invisible Writing* (New York: Macmillan, 1954) pp. 521–53.

3 Komsomol Participation in Education

In 1920 Lenin praised the Komsomol for helping Russia in her struggle to overcome more than one hundred years of backwardness. His wife Krupskaia was also watchful of the League's activities, especially in education, where she believed – and repeatedly reminded other party leaders – that the youth was a valuable resource in the battle against illiteracy. In 1918 she wrote of the 'extraordinary thirst for knowledge, readiness to teach by book and experience, which has seized the worker youth in particular'.[1]

The concern for education also dominated the Eighth Bolshevik Party Congress in March of 1919. There party leaders discussed the lack of attention given education since mass mobilization for the civil war. A resolution on 'Cultural Enlightenment Work' was passed in order to initiate the organization of 'clubs, teachers, libraries, lectures, meetings, books on the study of literature, and different courses and schools for social and natural sciences'. Lenin headed the delegation responsible for this resolution; his interest took the form of a question and answer session with Komsomol leadership. After lengthy discussion, he drew up a tentative plan for the League to attack illiteracy on the 'cultural front'. This plan was presented at the Third Komsomol Congress by an officer, K. Tsetkin.[2]

A party resolution at the Eighth Party Congress also designated the Komsomol as the coordinator of all oblast (regional) educational activities in cooperation with state systems and trade union organs. As tensions later grew during the First Five-Year Plan, this cooperation degenerated into fierce competition between League activists and the trade unions. At the time of the Eighth Party Congress, however, the leadership thought it was doing the trade unions a great service by placing part of the burden of responsibility on the Youth League.[3]

The government agency directly responsible for education in the Soviet Union was the Commissariat of the Enlightenment, identified by the acronym Narkompros. From 1918 until 1929, A. V. Lunacharsky (the Commissar), N. Pakrovsky, and Krupskaia headed Narkompros, though it is not clear exactly who was in charge. Throughout its history, Narkompros suffered accusations of disorganization, impracticality, and excessive sympathies for the old intelligentsia. With such a reputation, Narkompros was a favourite target of Komsomol criticism; the latter competed with Narkompros for jurisdiction in the school system and all cultural activities such as ballet, theatre, etc.[4]

The Komsomol gained genuine authority and power on Krupskaia's initiative in Petrograd in January of 1919. At that time, she proposed that the Youth League actually assume direction of educational activities by enforcing universal compulsory education. She hoped this would produce a significant rise in literacy among worker youth, since the Komsomol was to make sure all youth received an education, even those in the factory. In order to make education available to young factory workers, the Komsomol organized both day and night classes to accommodate different schedules. The Komsomol prompted specialists in Petrograd to open sixteen school clubs for worker youth, which were to hold extra lectures and discussions. Komsomol cells were authorized by the party to 'check up' on pedagogical personnel to assure the worker youth were receiving adequate political indoctrination, especially in factory situations.[5] This police power became a repeated annoyance to school officials and factory management. As more worker youth became literate, more joined the Komsomol. By February of 1920, the Petrograd Komsomol had the highest percentage of literate members in the country, including Moscow.

The Bolsheviks faced an enormous two-fold task in education. Not only did they have to teach a predominantly illiterate population to read and write, but they also had to create their own 'proletarian intelligentsia', a generation of specialists drawn from the lower classes of society. This creation of new élite became synonomous with the battle against illiteracy. In her comprehensive analysis of this process, Sheila Fitzpatrick identified a generation of young Soviets who, by making party goals their own, rapidly advanced up the ladder of success, in the process becoming a 'Red Elite'. Their climb to the top was not immediate however. The period after the civil war was one of transition. The concept of *vydvizhenie* (promotion) of workers and peasants into administrative and white collar jobs or higher education did not have a real impact until the First Five-Year Plan. Although beginning in 1918, *rabfaks* (worker's faculties) were established to prepare the workers for VUZy (university). Although it was potentially important, education of workers beyond a remedial level remained a relatively minor aspect of Soviet education until 1928.[6] For the most part, the NEP years involved a preoccupation with economic recovery and the logistics of raising the literacy level of the population.

In the 1920s, the Komsomol managed to represent the independent interests of young workers, especially in education. Although the League at times allied with Narkompros in disputes with the trade unions and factory management on general education and cultural questions, the Komsomol constructed its own platform which differed from Narkompros on virtually every other plank, particularly the emphasis on replacing old teaching methods with newer ones which would remove impediments to rapid advancement. The League not only criticized other organizations such as Narkompros, but actively lobbied for independent recognition from the party. The party made the error of not always taking the Komsomol seriously, and in fact chastised the League on several occasions for quarrelling with the trade unions.[7]

By the end of NEP, the Komsomol had made notable gains in the battle against illiteracy within its own ranks, but felt unappreciated and alienated from the population.[8] This was probably a realistic assessment, especially in the rural areas. Emphasis on improving the education of working youth in the factories had resulted in a lack of focus on the countryside. For League members, NEP signalled an unwelcome compromise, a degeneration of spirit and purpose. Although the League's role in education was solidified during the 1920s[9] (much to the chagrin of formal educators), youth as a whole was becoming restless and disenchanted. Society seemed even more stigmatized by backwardness and illiteracy than before the revolution, especially in contrast to high hopes for the creation of a socialist utopia. A cultural lag hung over this dream like a black cloud. As the government concerned itself with economic recovery, the standard of education again trailed dangerously. There was little spirit left in the intelligentsia and student circles, even though the country was slowly gaining economic stability. The youth may have been exhausted from the civil war, disillusioned with the Bolshevik government, or simply tired of fighting for ideals for which the rest of the population had no interest. The latter reason seems the most plausible. It was hard to remain enthusiastic when the majority of the population seemed caught up in self interest. Evidence of disaffection like alcoholism appeared among the educated as did an alarming increase in suicides coinciding with the death of the poet Esenin. Esenin cults appeared everywhere among the youth. The Komsomol fought against this degeneration of spirit by conducting anti-alcohol campaigns and promoting an image of moral fortitude.[10]

By the late 1920s, Stalin viewed this situation with disdain. Having announced a determination to pull his country into the twentieth century and to a position of greatness in proportion to land mass and population, he embarked upon the First Five-Year Plan with frightening intensity. Launching industrialization on a giant scale demanded labour, capital, and expertise in massive proportions. Stalin's plan required skilled people, a commodity still scarce in Russia. He told the Party Congress of 1928 that the belief that the peasants were incapable of achieving literacy hampered the training of specialists, and that the existence of élitist education which allowed the worker to rise above his fellows was undesirable. He told the Komsomol that it must bear responsibility for ending these abuses, and turn education around, into a practical tool:

> In order to build, one must know, one must master science. One must learn, clenching his teeth, not being afraid that enemies will laugh at us, at our ignorance, at our backwardness. Before us stands a fortress. This fortress is called science with its many branches. We must take this fortress at any cost. Youth must take this fortress, if youth is to become the real relief of the old guard.[11]

The message was clear: Russia had to modernize, and Stalin expected the youth to take the lead.

The Eighth Komsomol Congress in May of 1928 voted that the League should wipe out illiteracy immediately within its own ranks and that each literated Komsomolite should teach at least one illiterate comrade to read. By the Ninth Komsomol Congress in 1931, over one million members had been mobilized for the battle against illiteracy. This call was made primarily through *Komsomol'skaia Pravda*. The newspaper praised outstanding local chapters and publicized their contributions. It had played an important role all along. As early as 1928 its front pages con-

sistently ran stories on the building, renovation, and improvements made on schools in the countryside. Saturday holidays were
deemed Subbotniki work days, during which volunteer tasks were
undertaken by droves of eager young people pouring into the rural
areas.[12]

According to Andrei Bubnov, Commissar for Education in
1930, there had to be extensive cooperation within the educational
system itself so that education could be linked directly to the
Soviet Union's economic organization. This required a reorganization of the educational system; a transformation of all types of
intermediate schools into a single system of polytechnic schools.
This measure changed the existing programme which had not
provided any attempt at specialization until the seventeenth year.
The new system devoted the first seven years solely to 'general
education and a broad, general basis for the chief labor processes
used in different fields of industry and agriculture'. The goal was
to provide the student with practical knowledge to apply in diverse
areas.[13]

In short, the new system of polytechnic schools would allow
young workers to move more rapidly into fields of expertise, and
subsequently up the ladder of success. This satisfied the career
goals of Komsomolites and moved a large section of the population
nearer to becoming the much needed 'red experts'.

Komsomol participation in training the new proleterian élite
(themselves) had to take place after hours, on weekends, and by
correspondence course. The League could not sudsidize young
people to attend school full-time, but it did everything possible to
make course work available; this was most effectively accomplished through correspondence courses. Komsomolites nego-
tiated with scientific institutions, business and economic organizations, and technical colleges to arrange for regular assignments to
be placed at the disposal of correspondence course students. This
benefited non-members as well as Komsomolites, although the
chance to take better courses was used as an incentive to join the
League. In addition, arrangements were made for factory youth to
work in laboratories during regular school vacations. Groups of
students mailed their work to rural engineering–technical sections
for correction.[14]

On October 31, 1928, members of the Central Committee of the
party discussed the importance of supporting the Subbotniki.
They announced that Komsomolites needed permission to take

over old factories and equipment in order to create factory schools. Machine-tools, vices, motors, and other instruments were cleaned on Saturdays. The Komsomol procured the cooperation of nearby factory management to come in and serve as instructors. Lazar' Kaganovich cited an article in the *Torgovo-Promyshlennie Gazeta* (Commercial and industrial newspaper) which stated that work on such projects was not receiving enough assistance from the party in the form of Soviet Commissions. As an example of the favourable influence wielded by the League, Kaganovich went on to say that Moscow had responded immediately by creating an industrial commission to assist Subbotniki in the renovation of mills and factories. The commission reportedly began selection of criteria for a seven-year master's school to be conducted in newly remodelled factories. The Moscow committee also sent technical students on these Subbotniki in order to assure maximum assistance. As in all other ventures, the Komsomol was to organize and supervise the Subbotniki workers.[15]

One of the first factories to be evacuated and cleaned was a Baltiskogo collective factory in Moscow in November of 1928. This project was the beginning of a competitive ripple effect which was to sweep the country. Three to four hundred Komsomolites turned out on a Subbotniki to turn the old factory into a school where young industrial apprentices learned a trade while receiving an education. This particular factory took just one Saturday to transform into an FZY school boasting four hundred apprentices and fifty instructors.[16]

The Subbotniki system operated on a competitive basis, with *Komsomol'skaia Pravda* publishing the scores. A typical issue ran a tally such as this:

On November 17, 1928:
83 Subbotnika worked in Zamoskvorg, with
140 more expected on November 26.
1000 workers in Centrosoioz worked on a
Sunday from 9 AM until dark, earning a
total of 7,000 rubles for the construction
of a new school.
In the Zamoskvorenkovo region, 37 Komsomol
cells earned 22,000 rubles on a Subbotnika,
so this particular region came in first place.[17]

Truckloads of Komsomolites sang en route to and from their destinations each weekend, becoming the envy of any youth who did not participate. The Komsomol Subbotniki were held aloft as the model for emulation for the New Soviet Man. Propaganda lines incessantly chanted the virtues of sacrifice in building socialism. It is probable that the idea of acting on their own initiative and working long hours without the imposition of authority figures greatly appealed to many of the Komsomolites.

The League also performed a watchdog function, managing to step on toes both in the party apparatus and among its own membership. At one point the League newspaper criticized the party for allowing student scholarships to decrease. Focusing on the 1928–29 school year, the newspaper proclaimed that the woeful lack of scholarship money would result in 'poor academic progress and lack of proficiency' among new student workers, especially those taking senior courses.[18] Apparently the party did not bristle at this youthful insolence since *Pravda* echoed the same sentiment on student scholarships at the same time.

The League was particularly fond of admonishing its lower rank and file for not playing the game. Just as the newspaper heaped praise on those regions which met and exceeded their quotas, it was just as quick to admonish those who lagged behind. Not only was production level a closely scrutinized index of loyalty, but also the subscription rate of *Komsomol'skaia Pravda*. As the main organ of political indoctrination for young people, the newspaper was an important indication of correct political awarenes. All Komsomol cell members were encouraged to purchase the newspaper as an example to their friends. If subscription levels fell in an area, as they did in the Zshevskovski region situated near Moscow, it made the front page in the following fashion: 'In this region there are approximately 1,800 Komsomolites, and only 220 subscriptions of *Komsomol'skaia Pravda*. This area shows alarming disinterest and lack of work.' As a result of this exposure, the Zshevoskovski regional Komsomol quickly held a general meeting to discuss how to increase the purchase of the newspaper. The peer pressure within the League enjoyed enormous leverage in all situations that it deemed worthy of attention.[19]

Komsomol work in the sphere of education was not limited to factory training programmes in urban areas. The idealism which infected Komsomol members during this time was not unlike that of Peace Corps volunteers in the United States. The Soviet Union had many remote, isolated regions in which people lived in extremely primitive conditions. League members took responsibility for educating these people to be good Soviet citizens. This endeavour was perhaps one of the most noble and challenging of any in Komsomol history.

In an effort to unite the diverse nationality elements of the Soviet Union, the battle against illiteracy was waged in every far-flung corner of the nation. On Sakhalin Island, a boarding school was opened in 1928. Operating on a slim state allowance, a teacher arrived to begin his task with an allotment of 5 pens. His students arriving in kayaks and by reindeer included: 2 Yakuts, 21 Tungusians, 12 Giliaks, 6 Nigidaltsi, 5 Orochens, 8 Russians, 2 Germans, 2 Poles, 2 Mestizas (Ainu and Russian). An average day included academic and physical education in the mornings, and workshops in the afternoons. The pictorial method was used in teaching the Russian language.[20]

Other such institutes included one which was created in the woods of the former Alexandrov-Nevskaia Lavra Monastery in Leningrad, and also the Institute of the Peoples of the North housed in the Petersburg Religious Academy. The latter developed due to the initiative of 26 Komsomol students from Leningrad University. The students of the Institute of the People of the North included Lamuts, Evenkas, Samagirs, Negidaltsi Ezids, Yuraks, Uds, Golds, Kamchadales, Kurds, Tadjiks, Aleutians, Uzbeks, Baluchi, Tibetans, Buriats, and Mongols. There they learned to read and write and many became Komsomol members and carried the progressive wave back to homes which, in some cases, were a three-month journey by dog sled. These converts, along with the more hardy Komsomolites who ventured into the outlands, began transforming the taiga with such innovations as fishing cooperatives, fur stations, travelling medical and veterinary units, reindeer raising, alphabets and books, Red Tents (for political education), and radios.[21]

The battle against illiteracy made notable gains. In 1913 approximately 27 per cent of the population of Tsarist Russia was literate, while by 1930 62 per cent of the people of the USSR were literate. In comparison with urban schools and villages in urban vicinities, the growth of schools in remote villages was exceptionally strong. This was especially true in the Central Asian Republics such as Turkmenistan and Uzbekistan.[22]

The 'Battle Against Illiteracy' should be remembered as one of the more genuinely selfless, humane endeavors which the Komsomol participated in, one which truly helped modernize the Soviet Union. The desperate need to catch up with the west came from a fear of backwardness, combined with hunger for action on the part of the youth. This drove Komsomolites to educate themselves and their nation. The world was laughing at the Soviet Union, and this rankled Stalin greatly. His best option was to arouse intense feelings of nationalism and patriotism in those below him. This mindset was to infect the west in 1957, when the launching of Sputnik caused momentary panic and a reassessment of educational status in the modern world. Though the education of a population invariably complicates life, the process of doing so requires tremendous optimism and energy. By responding to this challenge, some Komsomolites secured a place for themselves which in later years would carry them as far as the Politburo.

Notes

1. E. V. Danilenko, 'Questions of Party Control Over Komsomol According to American Historians', *Vestnik Leningradskogo Universiteta*, 1970, no. 7, p. 40
2. Ibid., p. 40.
3. Ibid., p. 41.
4. Sheila Fitzpatrick, *Education and Social Mobility in the Soviet Union, 1921–1934* (Cambridge University Press, 1979) p. 11.
5. Ibid., p. 11.
6. Ibid., p. 5.
7. *Komsomol'skaia Pravda*, 1 Nov. 1925, 1.
8. Ralph Fisher, *Pattern for Soviet Youth* (New York: Columbia University Press, 1959) p. 79.
9. *Komsomol'skaia Pravda*, 23 Feb. 1926, p. 2.
10. Fisher, *Soviet Youth*, p. 80.
11. Ibid., p. 167.
12. *Komsomol'skaia Pravda*, Jan.–Dec., 1928.
13. On the Education Front', *Soviet Union Review*, 1930, no. 6, p. 92.
14. *Komsomol'skaia Pravda*, 20 Oct., 1928, p. 5.
15. Ibid., 31 Oct. 1928, p. 1.
16. Ibid., 17 Nov. 1928, p. 6.
17. Ibid., p. 6.
18. Ibid., 20 Oct. 1928, p. 5.
19. Ibid., 15 Nov. 1928, p. 4.
20. 'Pioneer Schools on Sakhalin Island', *Soviet Union Review*, 1932, no. 1, p. 16.

21.   'A visit to the University of the North', *Soviet Union Review*, 1930, no. 12, pp 191–3.
22.   'Expansion of Education in the Soviet Union, *Soviet Union Review*, 1930, no. 2, p. 66.

4 Collectivization

In a conversation with Winston Churchill, Stalin admitted that collectivizing the peasants of Russia into communal farms had been more severe than the first years of the Nazi invasion.[1] Forced collectivization turned the country inside out. It was a process of ruthless transformation in which the peasant population was coerced into providing the State with grain. Just as Stalin was impatient for the countryside to provide food for urban workers, the Komsomol was impatient for a chance to please Stalin. The League found a para-military role in collectivization, and made significant contributions to the achievement of Stalin's goals.

In order to understand the process of collectivization, it is essential to examine the role which Lenin's NEP played in setting the stage. The NEP has been compared to the period of degeneration of the French Revolution, the Thermidor Reaction. The purpose of NEP was to give the exhausted country a chance to recover; it was a period of compromise. NEP, as stated previously, for many young people marked a time of boredom, apathy, and extreme frustration. In 1926–27, a debate between the party leadership and Bukharin's supporters revealed that both sides felt the revolution was stagnating, and that the young people were becoming disillusioned. A prevalent mood among youth was one of nostalgia for what they believed to be the heroic days of the civil war,[2] and a desire to create such an intense and dramatic scenario for themselves. In 1927, the pendulum was indeed poised for a sweep, one which would result in the death and displacement of millions of Russian peasants.

Stalin's ideas on collectivization germinated in the grain crisis of 1928. He decided that it was necessary to establish Soviet influence in the countryside which would match that in the towns and urban areas. Stalin wished to end the dichotomy of a socialist sector in town and a private sector in the country. His remedy was to establish a powerful *kolkhozsovkhoz* (collective state farm) sector, and persuade the peasants to make the shift. Stalin's plan was practical in theory; it would be easier to force grain out of the existing 25 million farms if they were merged into smaller numbers of Soviet controlled large farms. The party leadership accepted Stalin's plan because they believed that this massive reorganization of the countryside would be done on a voluntary basis.[3] This emphasis on voluntary action precluded military intervention. The operation had to commence rapidly, and yet to send in troops from the Red Army would have been too blatant a contradiction. This is where the Komsomol participation came in. For all practical purposes, the Komsomol could function as an army. It was steeped in militaristic propaganda, organized, and convinced of the necessity to collectivize the peasants. In addition, the Komsomol had more influence in the countryside than did the party.

Prior to 1928, the Soviet government had little influence in the rural sector. Being an almost overwhelmingly urban party, peasant membership in the Bolshevik party approximated only 494 peasants and 4 rural party cells before 1917.[4] The Komsomol was the only substantial party support network in the countryside. By 1927, 1 million peasants and other young people living in rural areas were members of the League. Although this only amounts to approximately one rural inhabitant out of every hundred, it was the only indigenous support system the party had in the country, and was of great importance. Much of this support came from ex-Red Army men. The political education of 180 000 peasants who had been drafted for the civil war paid off greatly when they returned to their farms. During their service, most joined the party or Komsomol and came back to occupy leading positions in volost (district) and village Soviets.[5]

The party needed more influence in the countryside, and so the very nature of the membership in the Komsomol shifted accordingly. Prior to 1926, the League was adamantly opposed to admitting 'non-proletarians'.[6] The shift to embracing rural youth should not necessarily be viewed as the result of direct party pressure. The objectives of the League changed and coincided naturally with those of the party. Whether by its own initiative, or as the result of party demands, the Komsomol in 1928 counted 49 000 rural cells as compared with the party's 18 000 rural cells.[7] It was logical, then, that the Komsomol was a potential agency for carrying out collectivization. The Komsomol had influence and indigenous support in the countryside, and worked to maintain this position. At the time, the League was simply filling a gap. Later when the party needed to bring about Stalin's changes, the Komsomol stood equipped to do so.

In 1927 Stalin made a journey through the countryside, to

discover why there was such a shortage of grain. He concluded that the basic problem was that the kulaks (wealthy peasants) were hoarding the grain and thereby attempting to blackmail the Soviet state.[8] Stalin resolved to force a massive collectivization of the countryside, a campaign which would involve the 'transformation of small and scattered peasants' lots into large consolidated farms (kolkhozes) based on the joint collectivization of land using new superior techniques'.[9] Stalin proposed using persuasion and education to achieve this, ignoring the fact that peasants would respond to nothing short of increased material benefit. In contrast to the later situation in China, collectivization in Russia did not use self-interest as an incentive. The persuasive line was: collectivization for the good of all, not the individual.

Needless to say, most peasants did not respond readily to the notion of sacrificing their plots for the communal good. This immediately placed many of them in the category of 'enemies of the people'. Stalin's solution was coercion, enforced under Article 107 of the Criminal Code, under which peasant hoarders were to be prosecuted. Stalin's policy was clearly one of confrontation rather than conciliation,[10] a welcome idea to the minds of frustrated, bored Komsomolites. In the volatile atmosphere, Article 107 was the signal to attack, and the enemy had been targeted.

Prior to 1928, the Komsomol had been building its network in the countryside primarily through emphasis on recruiting membership and conducting political education. By the time of the Eighth Komsomol Congress (5–16 May 1928), the main task of the Komsomol in rural communities was to collectivize peasant farms. The Komsomolites were instructed to recognize the 'good' peasant as 'one who helps the poor', 'he who is for collectivization', and 'he who helps the party and the Soviet government'. Any peasant who did not fall into one of these categories was a kulak, an enemy of the state. All kulaks and their allies were to be expelled from the League. Any Komsomolite who was the head of a rural household, the Congress resolved, must belong to a collective as soon as one was established in his village.[11] It was during this congress that the first reference to Komsomol participation in collectivization appeared in *Komsomol'skaia Pravda*. At the end of the Eighth Komsomol Congress, Stalin sounded the battle cry when he appealed to the Komsomolites to remember that a 'few years of peace had led people to forget the enemy'. This notion greatly appealed to the Komsomolites. They shook off their NEP doldrums and prepared for war. Their mood virtually guaranteed Stalin's success with collectivization; he had found a 'multitude of enthusiastic accomplices'.[12]

During the battle against illiteracy in the 1920s, the Komsomol divided its efforts between the factory schools in the cities, and the remote regions of the north and far east. Although attempts were made to create Komsomol organizations among rural youth, urban members were not actually spending much time in the country. As a result, the urban Komsomol brigades which moved en masse to the rural areas during collectivization had no experience in dealing with the peasant population. This added to their difficulties when they attempted to persuade the peasants of the benefits of collectivized ownership.

The Komsomol was guided through collectivization by a succession of secretaries-general: N. Chaplin, A. Milchakov, and A. Kosarev. Among them Kosarev led the Komsomol in the setting up of Kolkhozes. Between 1928 and 1930, 5000 kolkhozes were established, with 93 per cent of all rural Komsomolites belonging to them. Kosarev also helped Stalin harness the energy of the League in 'building socialism'. Stalin knew what he was doing, and the extent to which the Komsomol effort made the difference between success and failure of collectivization was reflected in Stalin's obvious appreciation and recognition of Kosarev's leadership, when at the Seventeenth Party Congress in 1934 he was not only elected a member of the Central Committee of the All Union Communist Party of Bolsheviks, but was also inducted as a member of the Central Committee Orgburo.[13]

Beginning in 1928, the Komsomol began pouring into the countryside, attempting to convince the peasants to join collectives voluntarily and increase production. Partly due to Stalin's urging, these operations rapidly turned into military campaigns. Komsomol activity in the formation of kolkhozes took place in the form of group activity closely resembling troop movements. Each group was assigned a region, and ordered to deal with the peasant population in that area. In describing the exploits of the Komsomol during collectivization, as with other aspects of the First Five-Year Plan, *Komsomol'skaia Pravda* rarely cited a turnout of less than 1000 young people on any one project. Although it is tempting to view such figures as exaggerations, one must ask the question: if the Komsomol did not play a major role in the massive collectivization campaign, who did? The Red Army was the most likely candidate, but in fact most Red Army men were Komsomolites, as Chapter 2 has shown. Considering the general disillusionment of the young people in 1928, an attitude which has been repeatedly documented in Soviet sources as well as *émigré* studies, it is reasonable to assume that they did respond to Stalin's plan of action, saw a place in it for themselves, and poured into the countryside to fight on the grain front.

'Class War', as Stalin conveyed it to the Komsomol, was not 'an intellectual concept expressing a clash of economic interests', as Marx had originally defined it, but it was a real war of violence and bloodshed. His formula for victory was the liquidation of the exploiting class (kulaks) through class war by the proletariat.[14] In order to make this class war a working reality, Stalin needed a great deal of active support. The Komsomolites who responded to his call were convinced that they were participating in a cause greater than themselves. Their sense of mission was enhanced by ever-present propaganda. Stalin began his campaign in 1928, and it was full of militaristic jargon and catch phrases. An 'Open Letter from Stalin', one of many which appeared in *Komsomol'skaia Pravda* in 1928, is a good example of his rhetoric. In this letter he recognized the important role of the Komsomol 'light cavalry' detachments in the collection of the first harvest. These detachments were told to work under party guidance to develop a systematic plan for carrying out their 'partisan guerilla' work against the enemy. Komsomol committees were charged with studying 'manoeuvres' in order to deal with those villages which offered the most resistance.[15]

According to party line, collectivization of peasant households was an essential step toward the building of a classless society. The peasants were not sufficiently enlightened to understand the necessity of this action, so they therefore had to be 'convinced'. For this task the 'more responsible Communist comrades' were chosen to lead the fight. In colleges throughout the country, particularly enthusiastic and ambitious Komsomolites were selected to go into the country.[16]

The work of the Komsomolites was to be coordinated in each village with the soviet chairman and the local party cell secretary. In a general meeting the goals and aims of the party were explained. The disadvantages of private ownership and the advantages of collective ownership were emphasized with concrete examples. In party rhetoric: individualism aided the few at the expense of the many. In practical terms: collectivism allowed a greater reliance on complicated agricultural machinery, which in turn would increase crop size.[17]

Anastasyan Vairich was one of the more responsible Communist comrades chosen from the Leninakan Industrial Technical College. He and the rest of his nine-member team travelled by foot through the villages surrounding their school. Not unexpectedly, the only villagers who voluntarily joined the kolkhoz were party members and Komsomol members who owned land. In this particular case, shouting gave way to combat, which resulted in injury to the Komsomol members, and ultimately in the bloodshed of the peasants once the militia was called in.[18]

Komsomolites lost patience with the refusal of the peasants to contribute to what League members believed was the common good. Nicholai Lunev recalled his experience during collectivization. Lunev was appointed to the senior command position of a typical Komsomol brigade. The kulaks had interrupted spring planting to celebrate Easter. His testimony is an example of how difficult a Komsomolite's task could be:

> My assignment was to make a speech in the church during Easter service and tell the peasants to go out and start their sowing. I thought out beforehand what I was going to say, and as I approached the portal of the church I had it formulated in a coherent speech. But the peasants who were standing at the entrance looked at me in such an unfriendly and frightened manner that I was suddenly overcome with a feeling of disgust. I remembered the works of the chief of the Political Section and . . . became filled with fury against the unseen enemies of the Soviet regime and ran into the church. Nonetheless, the words which usually came so easily somehow stuck in my throat.[19]

Nicholai had left his own devout mother alone to observe Easter, that he might undertake a task for a political philosophy which he barely understood. His case was repeated thousands of times throughout Russia, as many young people encountered opposition from the peasants, and from within themselves.

Anti-religious campaigns began as an outgrowth of collectivization in the summer of 1928. Komsomolites roved the countryside closing down monasteries and exiling monks. This reached a peak in June of 1929, with the convening of the all-Union congress of the 'militant godless', which was addressed by Bukharin on behalf of the Central Committee. Not only the Russian Orthodox Church, but also any religious organization was ruthlessly persecuted. Roy Medvedev believes: 'The beginning of accelerated industrialization and collectivization thus coincided with attempts to root out "religious superstition" by force.' The 'Great Leap Forward' could not be hindered by dark forces of mysticism.[20]

Orthodox churches, as well as thousands of synagogues and mosques throughout the nation were torn down and destroyed. If Komsomolites initially hesitated to desecrate icons and destroy church property, this attitude changed as rapid modernization became top priority. It was necessary to destroy the old in order to build the new. To contribute to the achievement of this goal, Komsomol members were willing to sever their roots and ties with the past. Many of the excesses of the period of collectivization no doubt resulted from exchanges similar to that which Nicholai Lunev had with his villagers:

> Lunev asked, "And when shall we get busy with sowing?"
> "Sowing?" asked one of the peasants, "after Easter, of course."
> "And how long does your Easter last?" Lunev asked again sarcastically.
> "Some take a week, some two," was the reply.
> "But the crops will all be lost. The soil won't yield anything!" Lunev shouted.
> "There will be enough for us. We don't need much," the peasant responded.[21]

The peasants' attitude infuriated Lunev, along with most other young people in similar encounters. The natural consequence was an all-out war against the kulaks. As in most wars, there really was no right or wrong, but simply an explosive clash of attitudes and outlooks for the future. In the case of collectivization, the Komsomol became fiercely committed to breaking down the opposition. As early as 1921, the older members of the League carried pistols on long leather lanyards. This designated membership in the coveted 'Special Purpose Unit', an élite group which trained in guerilla warfare. Younger members were emboldened by the prospect of wielding power and authority at gunpoint, and aspired to such. The party did nothing to check these ambitions. Instead, the pages of *Pravda* quoted long letters of praise and encouragement from Stalin; no hint of disapproval.[22]

Although rural young people were caught up in what seemed to them to be a progressive movement, many found themselves in personal dilemmas. As college students came into villages and formed Komsomol organizations, a whole new world opened up to those living in the country. Many had been bound by the stifling demands of Russian Orthodoxy, and Komsomol membership appeared to them as a ticket out of their drab, ritualistic existence. This created family problems, as young people succumbed to mounting peer pressure and pulled away from parental authority. One Soviet emigre recalls:

> My parents categorically refused me permission to join the Pioneers or to have anything whatsoever to do with the Komsomol. And, presumably for this reason, both organizations began to attract me. My longing for self-expression was so strong, and the parental ban seemed so unjust, that it often came to family quarrels in which I would follow the pattern of the young heroes of Soviet literature and rebel against the wishes of my parents.[23]

At this time, *Komsomol'skaia Pravda* began a series of articles dealing with the advantages of life on a typical kolkhoz. One example boasted of acquiring a movie projector to enrich the cultural lives of the battle-worn Komsomolites in residence. This particular farm also included a drug rehabilitation centre. The article points out that 'drug addicts owe all of their adjustment to the cultural service facilities of the collective economy'.[24] In Pavlovsk volost, an artel (association for common work) helped maintain a school for the kolkhoz workers. The message here was that through the unique cooperation to be found only on the collective farm, educational and cultural opportunities increased several fold.[25]

In most instances, the introduction of modernization measures by the Komsomol did bring about a considerable improvement to the countryside, at least in the opinion of the rural young people. Typical projects cited by *Komsomol'skaia Pravda*, such as renovations of an old mill for use as a technical school, building of sanitation facilities, and the establishment of reading circles brought civilization to many backward areas. This had a two-fold impact on the youth. The obvious improvements served as a justification for those young people who were making the changes, and also encouraged others to join them. Stalin's plan had called for extensive change; the process of validation and reinforcement of the youth had a great deal to do with bringing that change about.

Was collectivization really a war, as Stalin said it was? If it was, then Stalin's rhetoric may have seemed valid to the Komsomol. Stalin urged the League to form Light Brigades and wage battle in the countryside.[26] If the Komsomol did meet peasant resistance to collectivization, then marching into villages in a state of combat readiness may have been not only fun, but a logical necessity. Although most scholars agree that discontent was widespread, there is a lively debate regarding whether an actual 'peasant war' or 'rebellion' occurred. Davies argues that official reports issued at the time are not consonant with the conclusions Olga Narkiewicz has drawn regarding the extent and nature of rural agitation. Narkiewicz declared that a full-scale 'peasant war' which reportedly occurred in the autumn of 1929, is in reality a misrepresentation. Apparently many peasants insisted on selling their own surplus, and this constituted some of the most active resistance encountered by the Komsomol. 'Black wagon-trains' (chernye obozy) frequently transported grain into the towns, in contrast to the 'red wagon-trains' organized by the authorities. Grain was often moved secretly in small quantities by cart in the middle of the night.[27] Violence erupted when the Komsomol disrupted such activities. When the situation warranted martial law, Komsomolites were issued arms (it is not clear by whom) and sent in detachments to protect such towns as Yekaterinovka in the North Caucasus. This area experienced an uprising of 2000 kulaks which began as anti-kolkhoz, becoming anti-Soviet in the process.[28] At many points the kulaks resorted to burning down cattle-sheds and wounding kolkhoz horses with axes and knives. Opposition was especially strong among the women, and in fact families were temporarily broken up when men volunteered for the collective and their wives held back.[29] Apparently the women were more steeped in Russian orthodoxy, and less inclined to change. This sort of active opposition is what gave League members a chance to fight a real war, much as their civil war heroes had done.

Although there was opposition in the Urals districts, the Komsomol was apparently successful in its efforts at land consolidation in that area. During the spring planting of 1929, scattered kolkhozy were brought together into unified groups. Whereas the regional and okrug authorities hesitated to initiate this action, Komsomol cells and activists of some kolkhozy, with additional support from the okrug Komsomol committee, managed to consolidate most holdings. The degree of opposition they faced is unknown. Although the central authorities in Moscow do not appear to have initiated this ambitious scheme, it received considerable support from Kaminsky at the Congress of Soviets in May 1929.[30]

Oftentimes the Komsomol would arrive at a village to find it totally deserted. One village in the Tatar republic evacuated its residents, following a rumour that 'communists will arrive tonight to plunder the poor and rich for the five-year plan'; a similar incident occurred after a rumour that 'the Komsomol will cut the throats of the middle peasants'.[31]

Meanwhile, the Soviet party leadership had become thoroughly embroiled in Stalin's hunt for deviationists. By 1928, Stalin remained in alliance with Bukharin, Rykov, and Tomsky, having discredited Trotsky, Zinoviev, and Kamenev. By the Ninth Komsomol Congress, Stalin stood alone. Kosarev (then the leading Komsomolite) and Kaganovich praised Stalin as the 'leader of the World Revolution', and 'the sole leader of the Komsomol'.[32] The League tried valiantly to follow party leadership manoeuvres, but just as it was beginning to recover from the emotional upheaval of the initiation of collectivization, the situation was compounded by an internal hunt for deviationists. The League faced perceived internal threats of 'Trotskyism', 'leftism', or 'rightism', as well as external peasant resistance.

Within the Komsomol leadership, formerly honored comrades such as Shatskin and Chaplin became deviationist quarry. Shatskin was targeted for copying Trotsky's tactic of pitting the Komsomol against the party, and supporting the 'right to doubt' heresy; he was thereby pronounced a leftist. Kosarev condemned Chaplin for knowing of others' deviationist tendencies and not fighting against them, or making them known to the party. This made Chaplin an accomplice in the 'Right-Leftist Bloc' which among other things:

1. denied that the last stage of NEP was also the first period of socialism;
2. questioned the rate of industrialization;
3. questioned the capability of the cadres to handle such rapid changes; and
4. accused the state of taking a 'feudal-lord' attitude toward the needs and interests of the peasants and the working class.[33]

The Rightists in the Komsomol erred by 'not informing the class struggle among youth', 'not cultivating anger toward the class enemy', but instead 'softening this struggle and cultivating the desire for everyone to live in peace'. Kosarev extended this to include all Komsomol organizations who sought to 'reeducate the young kulak in the Komsomol', rather than liquidate him as a class. For example, in *Komsomol'skaia Pravda*, the Nikona local Komsomol organization was severely chastised for defending and protecting its kulaks. Apparently this cell made the fatal error of petitioning Moscow to lower the intensity of coercion used upon the prosperous peasants. The scathing article denounced the unfortunate members of this unit, who probably had not followed events closely enough to detect the shift from 'convincing' the peasants to 'eliminating' them as a class. Everyone involved was disgraced, and the affair served as an example to other potential dissenters.[34] These embroglios kept the League too busy to question the events of collectivization. Members simply followed Stalin's orders to avoid becoming suspect.

Having set collectivization in motion, Stalin kept the youth motivated for the honourable completion of their mission. They were convinced that letting their enthusiasm wane would be a sign of disloyalty. Komsomolites ceased their liberal speech, and adopted Stalin's rhetoric. The good Komsomolite was to be unfailingly energized and committed to the intensity of class war and liquidation of the kulaks as a class. No compromise could exist.

When placed in the cauldron of collectivization, personal aspects of the Komsomol came to the surface. Komsomolites were more than soldiers in a make-believe army. They were individuals with idealistic goals for the good of all mankind, coupled with self-serving ambitions. More importantly, they possessed the energy to prevent this combination from becoming a contradiction. Stalin needed this kind of flexible energy to make the improbable process of collectivization a working reality.

Soviet youth went to the countryside during collectivization to follow their ideals, and to build socialism. Those who saw this process through to the end of the First Five-Year Plan were those who followed party rhetoric closely, and secured a place for themselves in the Soviet hierarchy.

Notes

1. Adam Ulam, *Stalin: the Man and His Era* (New York: The Viking Press, 1973) p. 290.
2. Sheila Fitzpatrick, *The Russian Revolution, 1917–1932* (Oxford University Press, 1984) p. 109.
3. Moshe Lewin in Robert V. Daniels (ed.), *The Stalin Revolution* (Lexington: D. C. Heath & Co., 1972 p. 79.
4. Robert W. Davies, *The Socialist Offensive: the Collectivization of Soviet Agriculture, 1929–1930* (London: Macmillan, 1980) p. 52.
5. Ibid., p. 53.
6. Ralph Fisher, *Pattern for Soviet Youth* (New York: Columbia University Press, 1959) p. 140.
7. Ibid., p. 163.
8. Fitzpatrick, *Russian Revolution*, p. 114.
9. Ulam, *Stalin*, p. 291.
10. Fitzpatrick, *Russian Revolution*, p. 114.
11. Fisher, *Soviet Youth*, p. 164.
12. Ulam, *Stalin*, p. 290.
13. Fisher, *Soviet Youth*, p. 164.
14. Ulam, *Stalin*, p. 318.
15. *Komsomol'skaia Pravda*, 17 Nov. 1928, p. 1.
16. Nikolai K. Novak-Deker, *Soviet Youth. Twelve Komsomol Histories* (Munich: Institut Zur Erforschung Der UdSSR, 1959) p. 65.
17. Ibid., p. 65.
18. Ibid., p. 66.
19. Ibid., p. 32.
20. Roy Medvedev in Robert C. Tucker (ed.), *Stalinism* (New York: W. W. Norton & Co., 1977) p. 208.
21. Novak-Deker, *Komsomol Histories*, p. 90.
22. *Pravda*, 2 June 1928, p. 2.
23. Novak-Deker, *Komsomol Histories*, p. 90.
24. *Komsomol'skaia Pravda*, 26 May 1928, p. 1.
25. Ibid., p. 1.
26. *Komsomol'skaia Pravda*, 17 Nov. 1928, p. 1.
27. Davies, *Socialist Offensive*, p. 84.
28. Ibid., p. 259.
29. Ibid., p. 125.
30. Ibid., p. 125.

31. Ibid., p. 85.
32. Fisher, *Soviet Youth*, p. 145.
33. Ibid., p. 147.
34. *Komsomol'skaia Pravda* 14 Dec. 1928, p. 4.

Conclusion

In *The Nature of Revolution*, Carleton Beals wrote, 'Like birth and death, revolution is violent change. Mostly an ugly process, it wears the visage of hope for a better, juster (sic) world, to achieve for which no sacrifice is too great.'[1] Revolution arises out of a hope for human perfection, and out of the belief that with determination and faith, Utopia is possible.[2] In the case of Russia after 1917, those who desired change had a formidable task before them. A wealthy élite had, prior to the revolution, sat atop a giant festering mass of humanity which was growing increasingly aware of its own discontent. This discontent gathered itself and exploded, manifesting in the youthful revolutionary generation of 1917.

Although it would be inaccurate to say that the Russian Revolution was carried out entirely by young people, this study has hopefully demonstrated that Russian youth did play a significant if not dominant role in that process. After the 1917 Revolution the youth became organized into the Komsomol, and essentially kept the revolution alive through the First Five-Year Plan. The Plan became a true war, and the youth felt they were on the side of the angels.

The role of the Komsomol has been woefully neglected in Western historical literature. We seem concerned with what happened in Stalin's Russia, but not with who made it happen. It is when revolution is viewed as an inevitable and possibly even cyclical phenomenon that the 'who' question becomes significant. This book concurs with the notion that revolution can be anticipated with the rise of new generations, for 'youth is born into a world he did not make, which bores him, hurts him, stifles him'.[3]

The youth of the Komsomol were no less than a disciplined body; an army, which fought for the successful completion of the First Five-Year Plan. As such, the Komsomol takes its place with such powerful youth organizations as the one which threatened the government of Singapore, dealt a death blow to the Sukarno regime in Indonesia, and succeeded in overthrowing the government of Syngman Rhee in South Korea.[4] The group which most closely rivalled the Komsomol in organized intensity was of course Mao's Red Guards during the Chinese Cultural Revolution.

None of these groups should be underestimated, but should

instead by analysed with respect to motivation and propensity. The Komsomol was motivated by the desire for change; no doubt fueled by adolescent energy and frustration. It responded to military rhetoric which Stalin used to his full advantage in the pages of *Komsomol'skaia Pravda*. It is important to re-emphasize the tone and techniques employed by the propaganda in *Komsomol'skaia Pravda*, and the fact that these were focused on creating an intense atmosphere of military conflict. Such an environment suggested opportunities for Soviet youth to achieve recognition for bravery and experience the glories of combat. By moving the country into a sense of urgency, Stalin created the illusion of a world poised on the edge of re-birth, a civilization about to be purged of its decadence and re-made along new, wonderful lines. In short, he made Soviet youth believe that through their own struggle they could help deliver a socialist Utopia.

Notes

1. Carlton Beals, *The Nature of Revolution* (New York: Thomas Y. Cromwell C., 1970) p. 2.
2. Ibid., p. 2.
3. Ibid., p. 2.
4. Peter Calvert, *A Study of Revolution* (Oxford: Clarendon Press, 1970) p. 120.

Bibliography

PRIMARY SOURCES

Books

Armiia i Komsomol, 'Molodaia Gvardiia' (Moscow: Progress Publishers, 1983).
Lenin, V. I., *Lenin On Youth* (Moscow: Progress Publishers, 1970).
Lenin, V. I., *Selected Works X* (New York: Progress Publishers, 1942).
Stalin, Joseph *Leninism* Leningrad: Cooperative Publishing Society of Foreign Workers in the USSR, 1934).
Stalin, Joseph *Selected Writings* (New York: Progress Publishers, 1942).

Articles

'A Visit to the University of the North', *Soviet Union Review*, Dec. 1930.
'Expansion of Education in the Soviet Union', *Soviet Union Review*, Feb. 1930.
'On the Education Front', *Soviet Union Review*, June 1930.
'Pioneer Schools on Sakhalin Island', *Soviet Union Review*, Jan. 1932.

Newsapapers

Komsomol'skaia Pravda (Komsomol Truth), Moscow, 1928–1930.
Pravda (Truth), Moscow, 1925–1930.

SECONDARY SOURCES

Books

Beals, Carlton, *The Nature of Revolution* (New York: Thomas Y. Cromwell Co., 1970).
Calvert, Peter, *A Study of Revolution* (Oxford: Clarendon Press, 1970).
Cornell, Richard, *Youth and Communism* (New York: Walker & Co., 1965).
Daniels, Robert V. (ed.), *The Stalin Revolution* (Lexington: D. C. Heath & Co., 1965).
Davies, R. W., *The Socialist Offensive: the Collectivization of Soviet Agriculture, 1929–1930* (London: Macmillan, 1980).
Deane, Michael J., *Political Control of the Soviet Armed Forces* (New York: Crane, Russak & Co., Inc., 1977).
Fisher, Ralph, *Pattern for Soviet Youth* (New York: Columbia University Press, 1959).
Fitzpatrick, Sheila (ed.), *Cultural Revolution in Russia 1928–1931* (Bloomington: Indiana University Press, 1978).
Fitzpatrick, Sheila, *Education and Soical Mobility in the Soviet Union 1921–1934* (Cambridge University Press, 1979).

56

Fitzpatrick, Sheila, *The Russian Revolution 1917–1932* (Oxford Universtiy Press, 1984).

Inkeles, Alex, *Public Opinion in Soviet Russia: a Study in Mass Persuasion* (Cambridge, Mass.: Harvard University Press, 1967).

Koestler, Arthur, *Arrow in the Blue* (New York: Macmillan, 1952).

Koestler, Arthur, *The Invisible Writing* (New York: Macmillan, 1954).

The Komsomol: Questions and Answers (Moscow: Progress Publishers, 1980).

McNeal, Robert H. (ed.), *Resolutions and Decisions of the Communist Party of the Soviet Union, vol. I: The Russian Social Democratic Labour Party 1988–1917* (University of Toronto Press, 1974).

Novak-Deker, Nicholai K., *Soviet Youth: Twelve Komsomol* Histories, Series I, no. 51 (Munich: Institut Zur Erforschung Der UdSSR, 1959).

Ostrovsky, Nicholai, *How the Steel Was Tempered* (Moscow: Progress Publishers, 1979).

Raymond, Ellsworth, *The Soviet State* (New York: Walker & Co., 1978).

Reed, John, *Ten Days that Shook the World* (New York: Signet Books, 1967).

Reich, Wilhelm, *The Mass Psychology of Fascism* (New York: Farrar, Straus & Giroux, 1970).

Sebald, Hans, *Adolescence: a Social Psychological Analysis*, 3rd edn (New Jersey: Prentice-Hall, Inc., 1968).

Tucker, Robert C. (ed.), *Stalinism* (New York: W. W. Norton & Co., 1977).

Ulam, Adam, *Stalin: the Man and His Era* (New York: The Viking Press, 1973).

Articles

Danilenko, E. V., 'Questions of Party Control Over Komsomol According to American Historians', *Vestnik Leningradskogo Universiteta* (July 1970).

Ploss, Sidney, 'Forty Years of the Komsomol', *The Soviet Union* (Feb. 1978).

Rassweiler, Anne D., 'Soviet Labor Policy in the First Five-Year Plan: the Dneprostroi Experience', *Slavic Review* (Summer 1983).

Index